BIRD

FLOAT,

TREE

SONG

DIS•ARTICULATED
POEMS BY
LOS ANGELES POETS

EDITED BY
TERRY WOLVERTON

SILVERTON BOOKS, LOS ANGELES, CA

BIRD FLOAT, TREE SONG

Manufactured in the United States of America.

Published by
SILVERTON BOOKS
4022 Fountain Avenue, Suite 202
Los Angeles, CA 90029-2220

Book design: Terry Wolverton.
Cover photograph: Yvonne M. Estrada.
The title is drawn from the poem
"What the trees know" by Donna Frazier
and is used with permission.

ISBN 13: 9780997314908
ISBN 10: 0997314907

First Edition

Dedicated to the poets of Los Angeles,
especially those who participated
in this collaborative poetry experiment

TABLE OF CONTENTS

INTRODUCTION

When poets sit down to write a poem, most of the time we begin with an idea. The idea might be rooted in an experience, a memory, a feeling, or a response to something we've encountered in the world. Then we set out to search for the right words—the best words, the best form—to capture that elusive idea.

That process began to break down for me as a poet in approximately 2010. My ideas were stuck in a rut, my language and images seemed repetitive. I would write a poem and think, "That's just so me," and I felt I wasn't doing anything new. I was tired of my mind and wanted to find a way to transform the way it worked when I sat down to write.

The dis•articulations process began in 2011. It pulled together different processes I'd used before with students—writing from prompts, "fevered writing" and "cut-ups." The element of sorting the cut-up words into their parts of speech—nouns, verbs, adjectives, prepositions, etc.—was new and seemed to reveal some previously hidden OCD aspect of my personality. The process of disarticulating the words was a stage of abstraction and helped me to release any connections I might have to the content of the fevered writing.

Here's how it worked:
• I would find four prompts.
• I would spend three minutes doing fevered writing in response to each prompt.
• I would "disarticulate" the four segments of fevered writing into their appropriate parts of speech.
• From these lists I would construct the poem.

I enjoyed the way these poems began without an idea, with nothing more than a list of words. I liked how using four segments of fevered writing, inspired by four unrelated prompts, guaranteed surprising juxtapositions. I welcomed the chance to see tendencies within my own use of language and to better learn the parts of speech (turns out I was especially weak on adverbs). I was excited to remember that many words could be used as multiple parts of speech—"clown" could be a noun or a verb, for example.

In 2013 I invited friends and strangers through Facebook to provide me with prompts. Each week I wrote a different dis•articulations poem and posted it on a blog, along with the prompts, the fevered writing and the lists of words. I invited the blog readers to write their own poems, and a few did, but not as many as I'd hoped.

In 2015 I was inspired to expand the dis•articulations process to a larger community. I created another blog and invited other Los Angeles poets to collaborate with me, one per month. My collaborator and I would begin by exchanging four prompts each. We conducted fevered writing on the prompts we received. Then we exchanged the fevered writing so that I would construct a poem from the words generated by my collaborator, and the collaborating poet would construct a poem from words generated by me. Prompts, fevered writing, and poems were posted to the blog.

Again I invited readers to write poems based on any stage of the process. This time I added a contest: The best poem posted by a reader each month would be awarded a $25 prize. The winning reader poems are also included here.

This collaborative process has allowed me to work with poets I've admired but not worked with previously and made me aware of poets I didn't know before. Working with words generated by another poet has been mind-expanding; each has taught me important lessons about what I tend to do and not do. One poet didn't use any body imagery. I always seem to have hands and lips and eyes all over my work. One poet's work is lush with sensory images. I tend to be more spare, especially in my fevered writing. One poet's work is dense with proper nouns. I hardly ever use them. One poet used relatively few words but repeated them many times. Some poets used words I would not typically use in a poem, and finding ways to incorporate them while retaining my voice was a great reminder of what a plastic material language is.

I'm grateful to all the collaborating poets and all the reader poets who took the dis•articulations challenge. I look forward to further explorations of our language, our perspectives, our processes of art making, and our poetic communities.

Terry Wolverton

How to Dis•articulate

A Note about Prompts

A prompt can be a grouping of words (two to ten words is a good guideline) that jumpstarts the imaginative process. For the collaborations, I asked that all words come from the media (print, broadcast or social). I highly recommend consulting sources you might not ordinarily look to for poetic inspiration: a cookbook, an electrician's manual, an automotive magazine, a feng shui handbook. The prompts scarcely matter; almost anything can trigger a chain of association that leads you to unexpected places.

About Fevered Writing

The origins of this writing exercise derive from Deena Metzger, who described it as "writing faster than you can think," and also Natalie Goldberg, who has used a similar technique as a writing meditation. The term "fevered writing" was coined by a former student of mine, the poet Yvette Beltran. This exercise asks you to write without thinking first about what will come out of you. You put the pen on the page, set the timer (for 3 minutes, or 5 minutes) and go. The goal is to keep the pen moving without stopping to think.

I like to work from a prompt, the more nonsensical, or the more unlike things I think about in my daily life, the better. You can use the prompts people we worked from for this book, or you can pull a few words out of any book. Don't over-determine it. The prompt is not your topic; it just provides a few words you can then bounce off of. (Think of it as your trampoline.)

Let go of any need to make sense, to spell correctly, to stick to any kind of subject, to write in complete sentences. Let the words pour through and surprise you as they manifest on the page. The idea is to bypass the linear brain and access the creative brain. If you are writing on lined paper, turn the page sideways so you can't write in the lines. (I have seen people do this on computer and even on their phones, but I personally advocate the kinetic experience of writing by hand.)

You can use this exercise in several ways:

- Use it as a warm-up exercise to blow the crust off your mind and begin to access a more imaginative voice;.
- Go back into what you've written, pull out a phrase or line that resonates for you and use that as the beginning of a new piece of writing.
- Do several rounds of fevered writing and see how you might begin to connect them in a new piece of writing.
- Disarticulate several rounds of fevered writing and use it as a lexicon to write a new poem, as the poets in this book have done.

Constructing a Dis•articulations Poem

1. Find four prompts.
2. Do three minutes of fevered writing for each prompt.
3. Disarticulate the four segments of fevered writing into their parts of speech.
4. You must select every word of the poem from the lists of dis•articulated fevered writing.
5. You don't have to use all the words.
6. You cannot add any words (unless you decide to cheat).
7. You may change verb tenses as needed.
8. You can change the part of speech represented by the word (e.g.,the word "flower" can be a noun, but also s a verb, as in "to flower").
9. You can repeat words even if they are not repeated in your lists.
10. The title must also be drawn from the lists of words.

Collaborating Poet: Jessica Ceballos

january

Jessica Ceballos is a poet, writer, designer, photographer, musician, community advocate and volunteer. During the day she helps to oversee the arts presentation space Avenue 50 Studio in Highland Park (her hometown), where she also curates the literary arts programming. Aside from hosting the monthly Bluebird Reading series she also curates Poesia Para La Gente, a program that brings poetry to non-traditional, but familiar spaces. She is literature editor of Los Angeles-based arts & culture magazine *YAY!LA* and she makes up 1/4 of Writ Large Press, a downtown LA-based small publisher; she also holds a seat with the Historic Highland Park Neighborhood Council, where she is chairs the Arts & Culture Committee and works to support policy and neighborhood development efforts that favor cultural and community sustainability over disproportionate economic advantage. Her written work has been published in various journals; print and online, and she has featured at various venues throughout Southern California, often times performing with musical accompaniment. Her poetry is also taught at Cal State San Marcos and UCLA. www.jessicaceballos.com.

January Poetry Prompts

Poetry Prompts from Jessica Ceballos

- medium brown girl.
- Do to others as you would have them do unto you.
- Less is more.
- Two Days, One Night.

Poetry Prompts from Terry Wolverton

- New weapon against superbugs.
- Mall closes after woman falls seven stories.
- More than 50 sperm whales, including mothers and daughters, visited Orange County.
- The future was such a long time ago.

Fevered Writing by Jessica Ceballos

New weapon against superbugs will just be another weapon against superbugs, against bugs, only making them super. Superior. What would happen if all the bugs in the world were destroyed? Do we need more weapons, against anything? I suppose when we make things strong enough to destroy us, we think twice, until we can make us stronger to destroy.

Mall closes after woman falls seven stories
I didn't want to be there the time he fell off the chair, standing up, did I say fell? I didn't want to be there the time he fell of his cliff, that time was way too close to call, way too close to where he wanted to be. Malls should close when people fall seven stories, so that they don't have to wonder if she fell on purpose, hearing them ask themselves that question for the rest of their lives.

More than 50 sperm whales, including mothers and calves, visited Orange County
I would like to trade places with a sperm whale, have her live in Los Angeles for a day, the day before she visits Orange County. Calves don't belong in Orange County, unless they plan on staying. Maybe the whales can stir the waters, make them digestible, taste better, and share the Orange County stories with their Alaskan friends.

The future was such a long time ago, she whispered into the back of my neck, just under my ponytail, as I was bending down to lock my hoverboard. It was the first time we went riding up this particular canyon, where I'd gone hiking everyday 30 years ago, when it was covered with grass and dirt. The city was called Los Angeles then, and Spanish wasn't such a rare language. From the top of this hill we would be able to see the downtown skyline, maybe even city hall. Funny how we thought we'd never see the day when grass was outlawed and "ethnicity" became a historical term. The future was such a long time ago.

Fevered Writing by Terry Wolverton

Medium brown girl in a dark blue world there is no happy medium we want to be extreme we want to live on the edge and jump into the sky instead we wait on this earth plane and if we're lucky it's just medium bad, though for many it's much worse than that and for a few it's just peachy that must be their karma to never have to confront their unfulfilled desires to never have to run through the streets screaming with madness no medium anything for them except maybe medium rare

Do unto others as you would have them do unto you One can do or one can be done to and that's the whole problem—there's no space to be and all of our interactions are based on this doing/done to model where is the space to simply breathe and dream, no one needing to prove anything, we could just look at one another and exsit and I don't need to criticize you or I don't need to get you to love me or I don't need to win the argument or I don't need to get you to do whatever it is you said you would do and we could be more like the dog and the cat.

Less is more they say, but doesn't that go against all the principles of mathematics, not to say economics? What if those who have more are just trying to convince the rest of us that they really have less, or trying to convince us that we're luckier to have less because, after all, it is more. They keep us so tangled up in our lust for a new refrigerator or the latest gadget that we can't see we have been robbed blind. Look at the beggar; isn't he better off with only his bowl to worry about?

Two Days, One Night
It used to be we'd have a night for each day, but now time has speeded up and there's no room for all that sleeping. Now we get one night for every two days and we just have to make do with that. Each of us needs to ensure we're completing the correct number of units of production and that can't happen while we're horizontal on the bed. It's been suggested we really only need one night per week, but the mattress makers got up in arms about that, as did the purveyors of cocktails.

THE PRINCIPLES OF MATHEMATICS

Jessica Ceballos

Not-so-simple economics is what convinced us to
look for the edges of this world extreme.
Though karma corrected our arguments,
we are allowed to keep loveless arms
from robbing the luckier of us.
The Problem?
We used to jump into the sky,
no one needing to prove anything,
completing unfulfilled screaming desires.
They said lucky, we said…blue.
Doing/done. Breathe
Now it takes two whole days
for the madness to run through this space,
to make us happy, one more time,
to exist with one another, for one more day.
Tangled/better. Dream
Whatever he said was less than
what each of us needed, to ensure…an us.
Dark/We wait.
The new mattress on the bed,
has been worse than bad.
Instead of trying to convince each of us to worry less,
we confronted those dark nights, for peachier mediums.
You and I don't need a we.

HOVER

Terry Wolverton

Years ago I stirred the future
until skyline fell to dirt.
I whispered an outlaw language
that only women heard.
I tasted the orange of the city
on the backs of their necks.
Every day we would bend and lock;
where was the place for wonder?

I became mother to the whales,
visited their seven waters.
I could stay under a long time
and trade funny stories in Spanish.
This was a weapon superior
to history; I could ask them
how they planned to foreclose time,
what the new world would be.

I longed for a chair in the grass
on top of a hill, the canyons
of downtown before me, digestible,
rarified cliffs and new malls.
From this place I could see
the after-years, when all questions
would fall back to the orange dirt,
when I would belong to another life.

READER POEM: NEW WEAPON AGAINST SUPER BUGS

Olga García Echeverría

It's tragic to be swallowed up by freeways
electronic devices & super bugs
I'm a junkie, a sac of water, blood, and bones.
My mind's a wild monkey
who has yet to read Thich Nhat Hanh
Sometimes evolution regresses
I used to come to poetry with so much want,
emotions bursting open. The word was my fist
full of flowers, my weapon
These days poetry eludes me
I wake up groggy with headline hangover
I'm covered in dog hair,
barking at formalities. Good morning my ass!
I scowl at Thanksgiving
hate White Elephants during Christmas
The neighbor's laugh annoys me
I'm a scrooge, a moody bitch,
a lazy witch who'd rather sleep than sweep
her flying broom across this dusty room
I used to…that's the line of the jaded…I used to
have cinnamon sticks & tuberoses
in my poetic mix
but now my poems reek of dampness
The ceiling in my bedroom had a leak
& someone's dirty bath
water came raining down on me
It's been weeks & I'm still waiting for repairs

for the Lords of the Land
to come examine the tiny hole, the slit of an eye

staring down from the soggy ceiling
(it could be made of tofu for all that I know)
My poetry used to apologize often
worry, edit itself to death,
it used to posture in positivity
seeking out lightness, beauty–migrating monarchs
hummingbirds with electric wings
but now it's ugly super bugs
that catch my eye
Like the winter mosquitos flying
drunk around the house, aimless
& void of gusto. When they land,
they wait, as if welcoming the end.
They're nothing like the fat summer flies
that invaded this past August. Those flew fast
& low, buzzing loud, swooping.
Bold as drones. Super bugs for sure.
My lethal weapon? The Sun,
a literary magazine rolled up tight
Ha! Poetry! I swung it in the air like a bat
Smashed it hard against the wall, windows,
ceiling fans, TV. It took hours of intense combat
One by one they fell, these super flies
Unforgettable was the last and largest of them
It was the size of a dung beetle
In the bathroom it charged at me
kamikaze style several times

Finally, I whacked it dead
(was that a smirk on its plastered face
as I flushed it down the toilet?)
Alas, poetry had saved the day…I thought
Until that bright morning when I noticed
the small colony of white maggots
sprouting from the drain.

Olga García Echeverría: Born and raised in East Los Angeles. Ultra Libra in love with the ocean and the clouds and the birds and the trees and the disappearing bees. Author of *Falling Angels: Cuentos y Poemas* (Calaca Press and Chibcha Press 2008). Teacher of English. Creator and destroyer of language. Splendid Spinster of the New Millennium who plans to joyfully spin words until her fingers turn to dust.

Collaborating Poet: Mike Sonksen

Equally a scholar and performer, **Mike Sonksen**, also known as Mike the Poet, is a 3rd-generation L.A. native acclaimed for poetry performances, published articles and mentoring teen writers. Following his graduation from U.C.L.A. in 1997, he has published over 500 essays and poems for a wide range of journals and websites. His first book, *I Am Alive in Los Angeles!* has been added to the curriculum of several universities and high schools. His weekly KCET column, "L.A. Letters," celebrates literary Los Angeles. Most recently in June 2014, he completed an Interdisciplinary M.A. in English and History from the California State University of Los Angeles. His next book, *Poetics of Location*, is forthcoming from Writ Large Press. Sonksen is now an Adjunct Professor at Southwest College and Woodbury University.

February Poetry Prompts

Poetry Prompts from Mike Sonksen

- Dying Shouldn't Be So Brutal.
- Gentrifying L.A.: Pick A Side.
- Save Us from Washington's Visionaries.
- How We Lost Track of Real Happiness.

Poetry Prompts from Terry Wolverton

- Judges should steer clear of the Boy Scouts.
- Record-Setting Balloonists Touch Down in Mexico…
- Ash Girl and Evacuation Warnings.
- "She was only a baby."

Fevered Writing — Mike Sonksen

Judges should steer clear of the Boy Scouts. Judges should steer clear of the boy scouts, there's nothing to say to the boys that hasn't already been said. The scouts shout about cubs and webelos. We be loyal scouts, judges cast doubt and talk about law and order. Boy scouts tie knots, they're not all that interesting when it comes down to it. There's more important matters for judges to attend to. Buy a box of Girl Scout cookies and keep things moving.

Record setting balloonists touch down in Mexico. Long before the airplane, man took flight in a hot air balloon. High amidst the clouds in a helium powered balloon, the aim was for the moon, the mission was to eclipse the horizon, the dream in the sky to touch the angels and say hello to God. The ambition to take flight started long before hot air with projects like the ancient pyramids. From day one man wanted to be more than he is. Inclined to rise to the sky, to move on up, the balloonists touched down in Mexico. They wanted to travel around the world; they set a record on their voyage.

Ash girl and evacuation warnings. Watch out for the ash from the volcano, evacuate the state, ash girl was almost blasted by traveling hot lava, stay away from Mt. St. Helens. Vesuvius is not new to us, Pompeii could happen today. Evacuate ash girl, it's a new world as cold as it ever was. Stay home out of the trajectory; the story of the volcano is older than humans. Name something else with the force of a volcano? Krakatoa cracked the Earth's magma, the tectonic plates always shake and there's no shortage of ash, girl. This is your evacuation warning.

She was only a baby. She was only a baby and did not deserve her fate; this is when life is not great. The power of hate overtakes the ugly side of many men. These men need to get in touch with their instability. She was only a baby, she had her whole life ahead of her, they need to find another place to project their negativity. She was only a baby, leave her destiny out of your own issues, the evil that men do is why we live in the world we do. People need to reconsider their impulsive behavior, she was only a baby.

Fevered Writing by Terry Wolverton

Dying shouldn't be so brutal, but why not? It's a violent collision between matter and the infinite. We don't give up easily. It takes a train crash or the invasion of the brain by cancer cells to make us cry, "Uncle." Even then the ego holds on. "Hold on, I still have more to do." And so perhaps we make it brutal through our resistance. It doesn't matter who we are or what we've done; the body will dissolve until even the memory of the body is gone. Still the earth turns. Tenderly, brutally turns. It's always been so.

Gentrifying LA — pick a side The sides were picked so long ago, way before you got here. You have to live somewhere and then you do until you can't afford it anymore. Even a flowerpot on the porch can trigger it. Being alive leaves its mark on the earth. We have a carbon footprint and we have the fingerprints of money, like a row of bruises. Someone has less than you; someone has more. The pecking order was established in the last millennium and there's no escaping it.

Save us from Washington's visionaries

What they see determines our reality and they can't see reality. Those gold-colored glasses they wear shape a vision in which so many of us are airbrushed out. I can feel my molecules dissolving as their vision erases me—the women, the queers, the artists, the thinkers, the not-wealthy. Where do we go once we've been erased? We live in a nether world outside their vision; they can't know what we're doing because they can't see us, but they fear our hot breath.

How we lost track of real happiness

It was just here a minute ago, wasn't it? Was it mislaid like my glasses or my keys? Did I put it someplace safe, like I did with my pendulum, and then forget where that was? I should never clean up. I can only keep track of things that are in front of my face. The minute it's tucked into a drawer, I not only forget where it is but often forget that it exists at all. This makes for a chaotic landscape, but it's better than the empty field of my mind when everything is put away.

WHERE DO WE GO ONCE WE'VE BEEN ERASED?

Mike Sonksen

We live in a nether world.
The sides were picked so long ago.
It's a violent collision between matter
and the infinite. We don't give up easily.
You have to live somewhere
and even then the ego holds on.

Where do we go
once we've been erased?
I can only keep track of things
in front of my face.

This makes for a chaotic landscape.
It takes a train crash or the invasion
of cancer to the brain to make us cry.
We make it brutal through our resistance.

It doesn't matter who we are
or what we've done.
Even a flowerpot on the porch
can trigger it.
The pecking order was established
in the last millennium.

We have a carbon footprint.
I can feel my molecules dissolving,
still the Earth turns tenderly.
It was just here a minute ago.

There's no escaping it, being alive leaves
its mark on the Earth,
it's always been so.
Those gold-colored glasses they wear shape
a vision in which so many of us
are airbrushed out.

We have the fingerprints of money
like a row of bruises. The body will dissolve
until even the memory is gone.
Did I put it someplace safe?
Was it mislaid like my glasses or my keys?
Hold on, I still have more to do today.

I forgot my pendulum. Wasn't it
tucked into a drawer?
The minute everything is put away
you can't afford it anymore.
We lost track of real happiness
way before we got here.

PYRAMID OF THE MOON

Terry Wolverton

She watched balloonists in the sky
and named them angels, clear warning
God would come to earth today.

"Our destiny will be eclipsed,"
she shouted. We doubted it. We
stayed loyal to our ambitions,

those ancient knots and boxes.
We wanted power. And cookies.
We didn't deserve judgment day.

Besides, no place to evacuate —
the old missions blasted, hot high
clouds overtaken by cold ash.

We steered away from the girl that
dreamed our fate. No shortage of hate
for her cracked and ugly stories.

Her trajectory will move her
to the Pyramid of the Moon.
Tectonic plates will start to shake.

When she takes flight she'll rise in
air, reconsidering this earth,
eclipsing the laws of matter.

She's only a girl, a baby
balloon; already she touches horizon,
almost longs for home.

READER POEM: HOW WE LOST TRACK OF REAL HAPPINESS

Shelly Krehbiel

So many lights. The streets are just vendors.
Time is a tree. All the prophets sat down
to watch it. Trucks came anyway, just plowed
them over. No need for figs or old words.
We started to build then, all the numbers
blazing, predicting justice in the loud
configurations of planes on screens. Now
is the time for action. Mercury stirs
his extravagant reflection. We know
the earth is round. We know how to turn books
into light. Isn't this beautiful? Soon
we'll make power from nothing, learn to grow
grass without water, catch fish without hooks.
No one prays. No geese will fly through our moon.

Shelly Krehbiel holds an M.F.A. from Antioch University Los Angeles. Her work has appeared or is forthcoming in *The Midwest Quarterly, Sulphur River Literary Review* and *The Fourth River*.

Collaborating Poet: A.K. Toney

In a few words, **A.K. Toney** is a poet, writer, educator and performance artist. As a World Stage Performance Gallery alumnus he had the honor to be mentored by jazz great, community leader and founder of the World Stage Billy Higgins. Toney's skills as a performance artist have taken him across the nation and abroad. His experience as a performance artist and educator has allowed him and his organization, Reading Is Poetry, to teach workshops with LA Unified schools, NAMI, and the Natural History Museum. Toney is also a contributing writer to KCET.

Website: readingispoetry.com

Twitter: @readingispoetry

March Poetry Prompts

Poetry Prompts from A.K. Toney
- Two Children May Have Died for You to Have Your Mobile Phone
- …yet the name "coltan" elicits quizzical looks.
- What makes anything worth having and owning has a lot to do with preserving art and culture within a natural environment.
- New City Election Dates and Schedules; One-Time Adjustment To Align Terms with New Election Dates By 2020. Charter Amendment 1

Poetry Prompts from Terry Wolverton
- L.A. inmate escapes from jail, is found in hot tub
- Prophet of Respect
- King of sea lions spotted in Southern California waters
- Scientists take the first ever photograph of light as both a wave and a particle

Fevered Writing by A.K. Toney

An inmate escapes from jail, is found in hot tub

This that cool warm relax with no caught up inside just flow like the dirt in this water but I ain't mud inside this houses without bars and sometimes I still feel locked up where there I's and air are still in and out like life never flowed from a delta inside a womb of concrete the home I never had inside where I want to become warm and massaged like I have no worries in the world jus this.

Prophet of Respect

They found him with the decrepit the sodomized the raped the childless the enslaved the victims the poor with the scroll of invisible a medal that shined from sweat of forehead because the nervous knew that when they came for the truth it was for live or die take or share but they never came with just respect they always fooled themselves in power

King of sea lions spotted in Southern California waters

I beached bitches, "Awrff! Awrff!" you heard me as I want for avocados instead of raw fish as the pier sits near take a picture dear human being look for me in the waters where no-where but your land is destination...

Scientists take the first ever photograph of light as both a wave and a particle

Random thought rays never seen. What is a star outside the dust that floats? I am but that dirt but a painting of actual glow caught in mist of life from image travelling is a view of time more than a moment, less than a second life

Fevered Writing by Terry Wolverton

Two Children May Have Died for You to Have Your Mobile Phone
And two rabbits died for my face cream. I gave up television but it didn't bring the turtles back to life. There are fewer whales because they are made into lipstick. And my car is causing polar bears to drown. Every step I take makes the world more dirty. I am consuming more than my share of oxygen. The sky has stopped being blue because I grow organic vegetables. Would the world be better off if we all just disappeared? Don't call me; I'm letting it go straight to voice mail.

yet the name "coltan" elicits quizzical looks.
I tried to change my name but it's like trying to change a shadow—the old one kept following me around. It looked so sad, like "what am I supposed to do now?" The name took the bus to Skid Row and wandered the streets with all the other souls that have no place to go, but it didn't fit there either. Its letters were bending and sagging, becoming unpronounceable, its sounds beginning to blur. So it came back to me, asked, "what's wrong with me?"

What makes anything worth having and owning has a lot to do with preserving art and culture within a natural environment.
I'm so weary of having and owning. My house is overrun with stuff and even when I give it away, more comes. Someday I'll be entombed with my stuff, suffocated with all that having. I don't even know what most of it is for. I long for empty rooms with blank walls. Let the art and culture reside inside me as stories, visions, dreams. All the materiality of it, its questions of value and worth, are overwhelming the natural environment, and making me so tired.

New City Election Dates and Schedules; One-Time Adjustment To Align Terms with New Election Dates By 2020. Charter Amendment 1

People don't vote and I don't think it matters what day the election is on. People think it's a big joke and it's all rigged and no one likes the choices they are given. People would rather go grab a sandwich or a beer, watch TV or take a walk in the sun. In Australia voting is mandatory and even if you're out of the country on election day you still have to go to your consulate and vote. Or they track you down and arrest you. Even so, the Australian government doesn't seem so much better than ours. Corporations run everything anyway.

SECULAR CRISIS

A.K. Toney

"What am I supposed to do now?"
So weary tired mandatory corporations…
Voting just disappeared, consuming share of oxygen
Blue stopped being sky
Skid souls wandered streets that row
Having owning stuff suffocated bending sagging
Cream rabbits for face
Stick whales on lips for Election Day
Polar bears drown and blur
Bring turtle's life to television
Entombed are stories visions dreams
Voicemail is letting go…
Big joke rigged with sandwich, beer and TV
Government track down arrest you
People matters is unpronounceable name
Coltan is more quizzical than organic
I take makes world more dirty
Art culture becoming world materiality
Car causing shadow, overrun stuff away
Reside inside your consulate environment
House the overwhelming natural
You me so better than ours
Change like trying to change
Choices are given rather grab and go
Walls with empty rooms worth someday
Value walk in the sun

Y'HEAR?

Terry Wolverton

I ain't the first bitch to travel
childless because I wanted to be King.
Womb's like jail when you're caught,
victim of a random, sweaty moment.
But I'm not fooled. I am no inmate.
I am the scroll of time, the picture
of power, particle and wave.

House of concrete bars—not my
destination. No locked world.
Scientists want to enslave the delta,
see it as mud or mist but
never flow. They rape my thoughts,
still I know my glow. A light being,
I shine with invisible stars.

I escape to nowhere, relax my worries
in clear air, massage my womb with dirt.
They never find me in this raw land.
My home is a spot in the hot sea.
I float just outside their view,
a lion on this decrepit beach,
a prophet of water and truth.

READER POEM: **TO HOLD UP THE SKY**

Sharon Venezio

To photograph light
as both wave and particle
is to steal the soul

of morning. Coffee
cold as you cup light in both
hands, like a flower

plucked from the round earth,
captured, consumed, eaten for
its beauty, until

at last it is ours
until there are no more stars
to hold up the sky

Sharon Venezio is the author of *The Silence of Doorways* (March 2013, Moon Tide Press). Her poems have appeared in *Spillway, Bellevue Literary Review, Midway Journal, Reed* and elsewhere. She lives in Los Angeles, where she works as a behavior analyst specializing in Autism. Read more at sharonvenezio.com.

Collaborating Poet: Angela Peñaredondo

Born in Iloilo City, Philippines, **Angela Peñaredondo** is a poet and artist. She received her MFA from the University of California, Riverside. Her work has appeared or is forthcoming in *The Margins, Four Way Review, Southern Humanities Review, Cream City Review, Tayo Literary Magazine* and elsewhere. She is also a VONA/Voices of Our Nations Art fellow. Angela is the author of the chapbook, *Maroon* (Jamii Publishing) and a recipient of the Hillary Gravendyk First Book Prize in Poetry for her full-length collection, *All Things Lose Thousands of Times.*

April Poetry Prompts

Poetry Prompts from Angela Peñaredondo
- Dis-Assembly Lines: gestures, situations, and surveillances
- A Garden & Honey Do's
- Secrets of Velvet Worm Slime
- There he was, sheepish and handsome on the elevated platform

Poetry Prompts from Terry Wolverton:
- At Pepperdine's Surf Chapel, prayers some in waves
- Herd of goats gets loose, chases children
- If you're reading this, it's too late
- The world's most oblivious driver lives in Canada

Fevered Writing by Angela Peñaredondo

The World's Most Oblivious Driver Leaves Canada.
It must be the closer one is to the artic. The white and black everything.
Here and somewhere there, only the goon chill and its people. No time
and all time for idleness. In zoos, cats grow even wilder. They are so
ready for death. Drivers aren't we all. Not knowing the story of our own
feet. Anymore. The underneath map of our towing. A dried mouth. A
piece of coal. Who owns our feet? And the road, what foreign road.
Strangers they've turned to. To hate this poem just as much as driving.
Drive me out.

If You're Reading this, It's Too Late.
The anthuriums have stiffened to statues on the ledge of my
dying balcony, exoskeletons only the super moon can summon. It is
weightlessness. A book becomes pigeon-holed, then a green mile long
and sky, sky. I have become wood. And the thistles today not reborn
into another invention of dirt. June has not come yet and you don't
want it to. Lilies, be your fingers and must you now speak of your
blasted appendages. Keep keys. The musical kind is what you want, not
the kind which opens. But a stuck, sticky hinged thing.

Herd of Goats Get Loose, Chase Children.
Let me be the sweet, blistered feet on something of want and
moving. Let me be theit iron horse, small and in three, precious parts.
Never alone with the sea rocks and dandelions. Charms left from a
steep drop. Let the wild cats chase me until I jump. Jump without
thinking. Jump from sharpest, weakest ledge, yes, needle-thin. Still it
does not collapse under my weight. I come at it fast and tear each wing
like a transparent petal. Eat and eat and wait. There is that toothsome
hint but do not mistake the sacchariferous for the weak. Blood is sugar.

At Pepperdine's Surf Chapel.

Somewhere up in the toss and roll, something from your world that you would call a far-off cast. It shook like Miles Davis but without autumn leaves. Sea salt has no room for that. No sway for that. It gives up to the marriage of light and mud like sardines in their thin slithering swim. Once I saw a chapel buried up by sea. What is left from doubt and Spanish conquest? It sinks in full like a boulder. Sometime the cross sticks out of the gray waves, thorn-like, covered in barnacles and sea mos. The road-side cliff brushes its shoulders jagged, paying no mind at all.

Fevered Writing by Terry Wolverton

There he was, sheepish and handsome on the elevated platform.
He was the latest to achieve sainthood. He had beat out several others for the honor and now he was ready to be ascended. There was a huge crowd gathered below and they were all taking pictures with their cell phones. He waved to them, a little nervously. It was only now starting to occur to him that he was actually going to be catapulted into space, and there was no coming back. He suddenly remembered about human sacrifice—wasn't that supposed to be an ancient rite, not done anymore?

Secrets of the Velvet Worm Slime.
People think my talents are natural and god-given. They don't know how hard a woman has to work to cultivate these kinds of gifts. If I told you my secrets, I'd have to kill you, because not everyone can handle this kind of truth. I didn't learn it from my mother, that's for sure. An old Romany woman took me under her wing when I was small. She saw something in me, she said, that shouldn't go to waste. It was hard to breathe in the fumes of her garlic breath, but it was worth it in the long run.

A Garden & Honey Dos.
The garden is an endless taskmistress, relentless in her needs. She will devour your sunlit days and still she needs more. There is always a weedy corner to rebuke you, a tree in need of pruning to shame you. There is always an invasion of insects to make you feel powerless. Bees come and buzz among the blooms, but they too are insatiable, always in need of fresh blossoms. They keep their honey elsewhere, no reward for you, only sweat equity and a sense of failure.

Dis-Assembly lines: gestures, situations and surveillances.

The women are being taken apart, their legs unscrewed from their hips, arms detached from their shoulders, breasts lopped off and put into jars for safe-keeping. The factory is busy; it now runs around the clock, enough work to occupy three shifts. The heat of the furnaces makes me sweat and at midnight, the line speeds up and they ask us to work faster. The foreman always watches, alert for any signs of resistance. The women must be disassembled and if we won't do it, he'll find a scab who will.

A VAMPIRE GIRL LIVES IN BAD CITY

Angela Peñaredondo

—after the film, *A Girl Walks Home Alone At Night*
    directed by Ana Lily Amirpour

What is first gathered, she disassembles
on the dry, insatiable ground.
Secrets she has taken apart
like little screws
from a dead clock.

One must cultivate needs
                     into readied heat, rekindled to breath—
alert without want of sun.

If not, then kill them, extinguish
what blossoms. When in the garden,
why prune what is already waste,
soon to be devoured by insects
& taken up by weeds.

How does equity keep
without human sacrifice?

She doubts the ancients, rebukes
any God-given things,
their quick, unnatural handling of power.

With Ease, she resists their sense of rites,

their invasions and talents,
their detached wings of thought,
their sweat and women.
               You don't remember wanting, she says,

those old furnaces like lines of jars, fumes
bottled for safekeeping.
What is worth keeping
until the end of your life?

No necessity to run, she occupies
the meditative buzz
just, like, that.

Elsewhere in corners,
she ascends
not to sainthood
but blooms into some sign of midnight:

an I
an underneath of Now
a being of Only
that finally rewards failure with gifts.

Minus any flash,
she becomes speed.
Through a crowd of others, her veil,
like a black wave of resistance: truth is a scab.

THE SPANISH CONQUEST

Terry Wolverton

That June, we'd been oblivious to the idleness of time,
blistered world shaking and swaying underneath our feet;
the herd was wilder then, until our blood stiffened, leaving salt
and thistles in our mouths.

I was alone in the arctic. I became Miles Davis
but without the musical light. I was sticky. I was stuck.
My world was full of strangers, thin and thorn-like. I'd summoned
them with my toothsome charms.

You'd been to the zoo and kept the keys. You let loose needle-thin
horses and weakened goats. It was too late for the dying cats;
they'd become statues, buried in dirt. Your fingers opened me,
hinted at greener miles.

Drivers, not ready for the road. So much invention and mud.
I wanted sugar, not coal. This was part of my charm. Chasing
poems, but not the story. The cross on your shoulders like a map
to nowhere, sunk in doubt.

Were we just not hinged for marriage, blasted chapel collapsed?
For a time we were transparent to one another, children
rolling on the ledge. We'd slither closer, but could not wait to
jump into the white sky.

What we wanted was weightlessness, as if on the jagged moon.
We didn't know we had exoskeletons, once we'd been reborn,
wings of iron that tore petals from the lilies that waited
by the side of the road.

READER POEM: GESTURES, SITUATIONS AND SURVEILLANCES

Jerry Garcia

Seeking my aura
in great big universes
—stars and matter.
Focus to epidermis
—particles, hair
and footsteps.

A stretch
and nod
clear cobwebs
of misperception;
the act
gives me pause
to assess.

Too many feelings pressure me
like percussive heartaches
fires of invention
fingertips scorched
with larceny
rebounding in holy
waters of tolerance

The embryonic gesture
of Kubrick's Star-Baby
stares too deeply
into my recalcitrant
asylum.

Jerry Garcia is a producer and editor of television commercials, documentaries and motion picture previews. His poetry has been seen in *Wide Awake: Poets of Los Angeles and Beyond, Chaparral, The Chiron Review, Askew, KCET's Departures: Poetry L.A. Style* and his chapbook *Hitchhiking with the Guilty*.

Collaborating Poet: Chiwan Choi

Chiwan Choi is the author of two poetry collections, *The Flood* and *Abductions*. He is also a partner at Writ Large Press, a DTLA based press focused on experimentations in publishing.

may

May Poetry Prompts

Poetry Prompts from Chiwan Choi

- Researchers Discover Fracking Fluids in Pennsylvania Well Water
- "Our Demand is Simple: Stop Killing Us."
- Russell Brand voted world's 4th most influential thinker.
- Here is the Face of Civil Rights

Poetry Prompts from Terry Wolverton

- Man punches bear to protect his per Chihuahua
- Home of child goddess unshaken
- If he says he's a woman, he's a woman
- To pimp a butterly

Fevered Writing by Chiwan Choi

Man punches bear to protect his pet Chihuahua.
And here's a partial list of things this brave man didn't protect: Tamir Rice. Freddie Gray. The handmade shacks in Nepal. My grandmother during her final days when we had to write her name on all her clothes so she wouldn't forget. Another person jumping from a downtown window during lunch hour. 214 pregnant girls. My bones that keep bending.

Home of child goddess unshaken while everything crumbles around it, but what does it mean to be blessed when all the walls that you'd embedded your memories into – the welt that the man from the church left of your 15 year old arm; the only photo from mother's youth, the one with the smile – is nothing more than a growing mountain that nameless people gather around, mourn blindly, walk away from toward a newer tragedy.

If he says he's woman, he's a woman.
And if he says I am ugly, I am ugly. If he says let there be light, the darkness crawls out of bed and leaves me without a goodbye. If he says you were a mistake, there are many alleys with mouths open to swallow. If he says he's a woman, what is my mother? If he says he is leaving, if he says you haven't tried hard enough, if he says stop by and eat, where do I find enough air?

To pimp a butterfly is no greater than holding my hands open in front of me to catch the rain. Nobody asks me what is my goodness. we assume thirst when we have waited in the sun for an April mercy. To begin a sentence that stops your heart in the middle of a sidewalk as three young people drop their childhoods on the cement and run past you is no greater than water drop on your skin.

Fevered Writing by Terry Wolverton

Researchers discover fracking fluids in Pennsylvania well water, but no one cares. They're drunk on money. That well has pesticides and chemical solvents and fertilizer and motor oil and blood and animal waste and the residue of all the prescription medicines people toss down the drain, so what's a little fracking fluid to add to the cocktail? We're mutating faster than we can understand, making our kids autistic, giving ourselves cancer; no wonder we get Alzheimer's. We drink to forget.

Russell Brand voted world's 4th most influential thinker. This redefines what it means to think. To think, one must be famous. One must be young and have a big media platform. One must be semi-hunky in a scruffy sort of way, and have sculpted muscles, all the while pretending none of this matters. To think, one needs to have a slightly sarcastic way of answering the reporter's questions, all the while seeming sincere and passionate. I used to think that thinking meant having ideas, but now I see I was all wrong.

Our demand is simple: Stop killing us. But who are we to make such a demand? Don't we remember signing up for this—to be the sacrificial lambs? They kill us because we are a threat to them. They kill us because they have lost their souls. They kill us because their god is a vengeful god. They kill us because they can. They kill us because, as they have imagined us, we are already dead. They kill us so we don't kill them first. We demand, but can we make our imaginations more powerful than theirs?

Here is the Face of Civil Rights. The face has been rearranged, the left eye shattered, the nose broken, the cheekbone disintegrated, the lip split, the jaw dislocated, the collarbone smashed, the windpipe broken, the right ear sliced off. They hold up a mirror: "Not so pretty now, are you?" but she looks and sees something else, something those holding the mirror cannot imagine. She sees her past and she sees her future. She sees herself dancing, dancing on their graves.

WAY OF ANSWERING

Chiwan Choi

who are we
that they kill us

redefines us
as motor oil and blood

don't we remember
one must be young

a mirror that cannot imagine
thinking meant having ideas

the lip split
mutating faster than we can understand

that we are
past her future

our imaginations
disintegrated

like cheekbones
and a vengeful god
drink to forget
dancing on the graves

all wrong
and not so pretty now

we're the residue
of the sacrificial lambs

signing up for a past
rearranged
shattered
dislocated

while pretending
no one cares
that they kill us
because they can

THE BEAR MOTHER

Terry Wolverton

She is pregnant with mistake.
She gathers photos—Tamir Rice,
Freddie Gray—everyone she did not protect.
Her sentence: To keep a list of goodbyes.
She tries to forget the nameless ones
but they crawl into her years.

Memories jump her bones, pimp her mercy
on a downtown sidewalk. Cement does not
catch her, church does not bless her.
Not your goddess, not your pet,
she swallows her handmade tragedy.
Her windows open to darkness.

Say her name with the mouths of alleys;
hold her with a hard old smile.
In her bed, the hours crumble,
this partial home of water, skin, light.
When you find welts on your arm
don't ask if her hands left them.

This woman thirsts for nobody.
She's not a child. Mountains
do not bend toward her rain.
She does not wait
for mourning to begin.
She will punch the sun blind.

READER POEM: RUSSELL BRAND, HE LOOKS LIKE JESUS BUT HE AIN'T

Tina Yang

Jesus appears in branded potatoes holding bread high
pitches snakes and fish across Pike Place Market each day.
Squeaks, "Hi! That's the man!" a la Robin Williams meme style
each time he wants a lollipop,
that's my Jesus and he don't walk on water.

Jesus sends the Dalai Lama an email each day of dogs
barking, romping across the meadows
they both giggle, snuffle and laugh, they're men.
They used to play the kazoos and kerfloos but now,
ah now, there's a drum to glam and YouTube to hang,
Russell Brand to man, Katy Perry to bang—
Grow out those pube hairs, girlfriend;
stand there streaming rainbows,
we all gotta spin dollars out of these dreams, baby;
Made in China dolls.

Tina Yang, born of Los Angeles, grew up in a Buddhist monastary in Northern California where her mother became a nun in 1987. She graduated with her BA from UCLA School of Film & TV, concentrating on documentary film. Tina has studied with "poet noir" Suzanne Lummis & is currentlya member of Poets at Work. She is looking forward to publishing her first chapbook from Arroyo Press.

Collaborating Poet: Elena Karina Byrne

A freelance teacher since 1982, **Elena Karina Byrne** is a visual artist, book reviewer, editor, lecturer, Poetry Consultant and Moderator for The Los Angeles Times Festival of Books, former 12 year Regional Director of the Poetry Society of America and Executive Director for the AVK Arts Foundation. She is also currently one of the final judges for the Kate/Kingsley Tufts Award in Poetry, a Contributing Editor for the *Los Angeles Review of Books,* and Literary Programs Director for The Ruskin Art Club.She sits on the advisory boards for What Books and White Pine Press. Elena received the 2015 Distinguished Service Award from Beyond Baroque's Literary Arts Center.

Elena was part of the West Hollywood Book Fair's Planning Committee and worked with Red Car studios editing several documentary film projects including *The Big Read, Muse of Fire* and *Why Shakespeare?* Since 1991 Elena has organized or funded programs for the Museum of Contemporary Art, the University of Southern California's Doheny Memorial Library, the Getty Research Institute at the J. Paul Getty Center, UCLA's CAP/Center for the Art of Performance, Columbia University's School of the Arts International Translation Project, CAFAM's Poetry and Art Collaboration Series, The

Metropolitan Transit Authority's Metro Art live Poetry in Motion annual readings, and the renowned Chateau Marmont "Act of the Poet" series. She was the 2005 Poetry Co-Editor for *The Los Angeles Review* and one of three judges for the 2006 PEN USA Literary Award in Poetry.

Her book reviews and essays have appeared in *Slope, Poetry International, The Journal* and *Oniverse.* Elena's publications, among others, include *2009 Pushcart Prize XXXIII Best of the Small Presses, Best American Poetry 2005, The Yale Review, The Paris Review, American Poetry Review, The Kenyon Review, Ploughshares, Poetry, TriQuarterly, Colorado Review, Denver Quarterly, Dublin Poetry Review, Levurelitteraire, Painted Bride Quarterly , Barrow Street, Volt, Antioch Review, Massachusetts Review, Verse, The Journal, Hotel Amerika, Pool, Crazyhorse, Prairie Schooner, Verse, Drunken Boat, The Offending Adam, Anthology of Magazine Verse & Yearbook of American Poetry, Breathe: 101 Contemporary Odes, Bear Flag Republic: Prose Poems and Poetics From California, Wide Awake: Poets of Los Angeles and Beyond, Poetry Daily Anthology,* and *Spunk and Bite: A Writer's Guide to Punchier, More Engaging Language and Style.* Books include: *The Flammable Bird* (Zoo Press/Tupelo Press 2002), *Masque,* (Tupelo Press 2008) and *Squander (Omnidawn 2016);* she just completed a book of essays, *Voyeur Hour: Meditations on Poetry, Art and Desire.*

June Poetry Prompts

Poetry Prompts from Elena Karina Byrne

- …low energy transfer orbits to the Japanese lunar
- An Iceberg Flipped Over, and Its Underside Is Breathtaking
- DOUBLE GAME
- Birthday Cake Shot

Poetry Prompts from Terry Wolverton

- Sundown Over Ghost Town
- Set Yourself on Fire
- Lions Don't Eat Us
- Abandoned Detroit Home Filled with Thousands of Flowers

Fevered Writing by Elena Karina Byrne

Prompt: Set Yourself On Fire

Set Yourself On Fire

Goodbye—
On fire set and selfsame sorrow's
soot and tinder-making and making

you into night's bonfire bride of bed mattresses thrown
from the windows, white sheet Spanish sails in surrender

as if, as if carried off from that last thing you wanted
yourself consumed by, the last borrowed air taken

from the ashen mirror's aged face forgetting you every time
you left the room, every time the house

tooth and nail, two-by-four splinter
falls down back into the marriage ground, blackened,
tongue-tied by time and time again

until you can't see, burning from inside out, beehive-alight:
red dress, flame ribbons, dissolving paper shoes,
shame on you.

Prompt: Lions Don't Eat Us

No, Don't

Stanley Kunitz said the thing that eats the heart is mostly heart and I
wish, there in the blue blossom-backwards garden I was hungry,
so hungry in someone's arms again, afraid in full open mouth-desire.
I wish I knew where I put my fear, my childhood, sitting in the past,
it's zoo, sitting on the winding Escher stairs, saying this outloud
to my dead mother, so loud a lion's head in the mouth loud
caught audience breath for breath measure making us sad when we go
home to say it to the father, you, dead in the heart and alone
because they are all gone and can't feed you anymore;
you can't sit in the lap, on the mouth, kneeling on the floor;
you can't sit in the cement highchair, sit in the room
with the lion who won't eat you, who won't eat me, facing
the garden, his yellow haystack head shaking.

**Prompt: Abandoned Detroit Home Filled with Thousands of
Flowers**

Home Filled with Thousands of Flowers

so many flowers you couldn't breathe coming in
the front door, fallen and rising, lilac-bruised and picked and plucked
fresh, slipping hothouse skins, hot-headed-red over green, spring's
temper tantrum in silence for this... wedding funeral, abandoned
sweet constellation,

petals large and small, stem and stamen, torn softly, each
severed pink and yellow head where the missing bed is now,
missing moon table and chairs replaced with so many mouths,

but see there over the fireplace mantle its invisible family portrait, all
Impatience over Peony, the private parts of field Lavender are chained
around the ankles of the children no longer here.

Bathtub filled with so many sunflowers, wedding names for herb rows.
What happens in Detroit, thousand mouse corsage, dust lintel and
    moldings,
greening their perfume, still wet in prayer along the stained corridor,
    seed nails
driven away from open sky, when you empty the first home, its roof
    gone?

Prompt: Sundown Over Ghost Town

Palm Springs, Pale as a Church Candle

You can't see sundown, where you're going fast.
You can't see over the wood steering wheel.
You drive and drive and drive away from the shining shore and
holy smell of her, ghost in a town of ghosts driven.
Giant white windmills ache and cut, ache over
the hills and through the fields, grandmother's ghosthouse
small in the distance until the hot road brings the water
back, rising up mirage black from the blacktop,
a nun's habit horizon disappearing as you near.
Desert mountains, fallen politics, last cowboy cactus
and dry rock and rock thrown centuries ago,
your cowboy hat flattened under the pillow until you
wake up over the edge of the canyon, the horsehair bed
tipping its scales, imaginary gun in your hand,
your head, one starving coyote running...

Fevered Writing by Terry Wolverton

birthday cake shot

It was a not untypical white trash holiday gathering, everyone shitfaced and argumentative, and ending with a bullet in the middle of the cake. The cake bled raspberry sauce onto the white tablecloth and everyone was quiet for a moment. But only a moment. Everyone forgot about the cake except the girl whose birthday it was, but they had forgotten about her too, left sitting by herself at the wrecked table while two uncles punched each other in the face and an aunt started screaming.

...low energy transfer orbits to the Japanese lunar

I want to plug myself in to get the energy transfer. I've been feeling kinda peekid, pale and anemic, as if my life force needs a booster shot, and that's when I heard about energy transfer, how someone with too much energy will download it into someone who needs more, like a blood transfusion, but it's a great way to invigorate. Choice of donor is key–I don't want some road rage testosterone maniac who's going to make me yell at my boss and lose my job.

An Iceberg flipped over and its underside is breathtaking

Its underside is breathing, taking oxygen for the first time. It's spent its life in water and now it turns toward the sun. The iceberg begins to release what's long been trapped beneath its frozen surface–fossils and bones and stones and fish and darkness. It will lose everything. Its solidity becomes fluid and then seeds attach to its mass and begin to grow. In a few months there's will be moss and tiny flowers that create a new perfume in the atmosphere. Somewhere, scientists are mourning this development but the iceberg celebrates its metamorphosis.

Double Game is too tame I had no shame it's really lame the triple quadruple Game, that's my name but players gotta play and so I take the first leap onto the hopscotch squares and my hoola-hoop is spinning around my hips and I'm jumping the rope that two girls are patiently twirling. How can I not win but what does it even mean to win, will I get the big red heart or the stuffed panda or will I get both because it's a double game or will it end in flames as I spontaneously Combust over the Stadium and will someone start singing the anthem for me?

DOUBLE GAME: FACE SHOT

Elena Karina Byrne

I. Metamorphosis: Everyone Was

Quiet. Yell.
There will be road rage and stones, a few
months forgotten in each other,
lease of two who need more.
Taking double oxygen turns, I will lose everything.
There will be white tablecloth moss and tiny cake
flowers. But only a moment
will I get that big red heart, choice
 of donor, mourning a booster shot-start in flames,
energy transfer, too much energy…
spontaneous testosterone seed.

Now: Who more tame and spent—
fossil job boss, sitting maniac, scientists over an iceberg—
who's going to make me me,
an anthem for me? (Two sunsauce girls?)
Double game orbit. Lunar fluid-
feeling over the head, twirling. This too I take to mean
something is gathering to invigorate both players for
a moment. It is. It was. But
to win was a forced will of forgetting
about her.

II. The Beginning Too: Her-self, My-self

But I don't want trash game, hopscotch choice-play, to start
singing the girl holiday, don't want need, sauce hoola-hoop, don't
want (bullet shame in wanting) to combust over

the great way darkness, its frozen stadium
in the middle trapped… In the somewhere, this
spinning in, first leap onto, ending with, — this
heard-about jumping left and left, left toward
the Japanese square to stand in as if
my life, its underside water (fish-breathing by herself begins)
celebrates my birthday pekid end.

Because, like a two uncle blood transfusion,
the stuffed cake bled raspberry sauce
and an aunt started screaming a shit-faced key in C
toward the perfume sun…
the wrecked table, its frozen, pale surface,
everyone ending there, forgotten, in the flipped over
face-place, myself, argumentative and anemic,
what's long been a taking under-side,
untypical family seed of myself
laid in the solid ground's iceberg where my name
(how someone becomes)
then shame-played around my hips,
that tame-time Panda patience punched
out of you/me. Because of this
long attach-kind of development, it forces breathing, bones
to grow, cake mass to quadruple, forces you to get even,
to release the fluid rope of spent names
when jumping onto/in/under the water…
that underside other anthem game, the kind of great
feeling you get into when, beneath
breathtaking shots of the dark, you both
can birthday yourself for a first time
in the picture.

BORROWED CORSAGE

Terry Wolverton

My mother blackened sunflowers
with her temper; hands splintered dry
stems of lavender, tipped over
the beehive. A lion bride, she
wanted an audience. She threw
her wedding dress into the fireplace,
said her marriage was a nail
in her heart, a funeral for
her sad, invisible childhood.

My coyote father plucked red
ribbons from the flames, carried his
mattress to the horizon, caught
the last prayer of sundown. We
saw him as a constellation,
tinder in the night sky, burning
roof over our heads. When we no
longer saw him, we forgot him
for centuries, an empty mirror.

I was the family ghost, starved
for the moon; a peony set
in soot; nun who knelt by
abandoned windmills. Every
room in the fallen house breathed with
impatience, bathtub filled with
names of the missing. Shiny gun

under the pillow blossomed into
the hungry politics of shame.

In the hothouse, my pink hat aches;
light surrenders to wet silence.
My white teeth shake your lintel, fill
the green corridor. And you, my
cowboy, in your petalled dress, what
will you say to me in tongue-tied
Spanish? Will you bruise the lilacs
of desire, stain my skin holy
with the still-hot ashes of spring?

READER POEM: TREASURE HUNT

Donna Prinzmetal

I want to dig in my garden under the tomatoes through the cities of earthworms and find a map. I want the map to be quiet and torn and have the impossible marked on it: everything luminous and easy to find. I can look on the wrinkled paper, yellowed and uneven as skin even after all the ablutions. I can hear the jukebox playing "Crazy" over and over while the couple wraps themselves around each other for a dance slower than slow. And there, just to the left, is the abandoned house filled with thousands of flowers, relics of an apology no one believed. On the map you can see the secret passage behind the dresser, the place the stars slid off of the mobile, as the baby reached for them, the grandfather clock stuck at 10:17 with no working second hand but a sturdy insistent heartbeat you can almost hear through the skin of the map. What grows there under the bridge, behind the mimosa trees, what grows under the claw fence, beneath the sludge of that underwater garden? There is a small silvery thing, you can barely hear it, a canticle, a moment that undresses itself until your only company is amnesia, and that's on the map too, that mishap of memory. Let me find that place on the map where a rivulet of water sluices down the window, but not just any window, the window with an eagle just on the other side and on the map you can see that lilac scented garden bustling with bees. I'm sorry to tell you this is not my home. I'm out there where the urchins hide, behind the mirror. On the map I can see where my skin used to be, when I had skin, when I had a beginning and a middle. Each object you meet on the map, refuses to be found anywhere else, in midair, in what you might assume is the "real world" but you would be wrong.

Donna Prinzmetal is a poet, psychotherapist and teacher. She has taught poetry and creative writing for over twenty-five years to adults and children. Donna often uses writing to facilitate restoration and healing in her psychotherapy practice. Her poems have appeared in many magazines including: *Prairie Schooner, The Oregonian, The Comstock Review,* and *The Journal. Snow White, When No One Was Looking* was published in May of 2014 by CW Books, an imprint of WordTech Communications. This is a book of persona poems in which Snow White speaks, often in a contemporary voice, and includes multiple versions of the fairy tale. It is Donna's first book.

Collaborating Poet: Olga García Echeverría

Olga García Echeverría is the author of *Falling Angels: Cuentos y Poemas.* Her work has been published in *Lavandería: A Mixed Load of Women, Wash, and Words, U.S. Latino Literature Today, Telling Tongues: A Latin@ Anthology on Language, The Sun Magazine,* and is forthcoming in *Jota* by Kórima Press. She was selected by A Room of Her Own (AROHO) as the 2013 Touching Lives Fellow, and in the spring of 2015 she was a finalist for AROHO's Orlando Literary Prize in the genre of Creative Non-fiction. She lives, teaches, and shape-shifts in Los Angeles.

July Poetry Prompts

Poetry Prompts from Olga García Echeverría
- Woman Gives Birth, Fights Off Bees, Starts Wild Fire in Northern California
- What Gaining a Leap Second Means For a Hummingbird
- Trust Me. Butter is Better.
- Goldfish the Size of Dinner Plates Are Multiplying Like Bunnies

Poetry Prompts from Terry Wolverton
- Space is hard
- Dolphin leaps onto boat, injuring woman
- Poetry is against gravity
- Guns in Paradise

Fevered Writing by Olga Garcia Echeverría

Space is hard to decipher. Whenever I try to be an atheist, I look up and get baffled by things I cannot see, like moons made of ice. Jupiter's menstrual red hot spots. La Luna's fierce chalky gray cratered face. The Milky Way—fuck! Space is hard, but I imagine it soft, plush to the touch, a down pillow wrapped in silk, cold, littered with glitter, metallic dark blues. Space is hard, but I imagine it liquid, the blackest of oceans with infinite depths.

Dolphin leaps onto boat, injuring woman…and sharks that keep attacking people at the beach baffle scientists. Last time I walked along the shore, I spotted/dodged black rubbery oil spill blobs. Charred jellyfish. Dead seagull. Plastic water bottle(s). Amber seaweed. Scattered red and yellow long stem roses, altar to the sea.

Poetry is against gravity. A haiku, so small boned, can weigh 1000 pounds. It rains upward. We all become unanchored to the surface of the earth and spin like dirty laundry into space. Freeways melt into mercury rivers. Snow hardens in the sun. Space space space is a breath, an opening of the mouth, the beginning of a kiss, or a final good-bye, gasp. It's the slit of an eye, an ocean in my heart, hot hot pink, translucent amethyst purple. I went to the Falls and saw ghosts in the mist. I went to the Falls and saw ghosts in the mist.

Guns in Paradise—you can take it with you, you know, your gun because God, like us, loves guns and it's sad to say but even in Paradise its good to be armed. Nowadays they're kinda letting everyone into Heaven, those homos, for example, what with the legalization of marriage, first it's Civil, then it's Church, then, mark my words, it's Heaven. Even women who've had abortions are being let in. Paradise used to be like, like…well, like Hawaii (minus all the native Hawaiians, of course, since they're pagans), like that but with a shit load of guns. Now it's gone to shit, but I hear it ain't all bad. You know in Paradise, you can hunt freely, no permits needed, no animal rights organizations (at least not yet), just you, you, you, and your badass guns to shoot shoot shoot…

Fevered Writing by Terry Wolverton

Trust me. Butter is better than spackle on your sandwich, id better than motor oil on your toast, is better than hair gel on your waffle. Butter is one of only a few foods that is yellow and yellow is the color associated with the navel chakra. One's chakras need to be vibrating, the wheels spinning so the energy can circulate throughout the system. Only then can we trust. The safest place to be is inside your own, strong energy field, my yoga teacher used to say. Maybe no place else is safe at all. The butter drips from my fingers.

Woman gives birth, fights off bees, starts wildfire in Northern California. Yeah, yeah, yeah, we all have such busy lives. My day started cleaning up dog diarrhea. That was before I had to go to the DMV. But no one is writing a newspaper article about me. It doesn't pay to give birth these days. The planet is already overcrowded, the freeways are a nightmare, and bees are being eradicated by pesticides so soon there won't be any food for any of us. Why not start a wildfire? It makes as much sense as anything.

What gaining a leap second means for a hummingbird. Just last week my friend was complaining that she needed more time. Then– bam! They stuck another second on the universal clock. How they did this, I'm not sure–and where I spent that second I can't recall–probably on Facebook or something. Or maybe I took an extra second to look into your eyes and saw some softness there for the first time in a long time. Or maybe I slept in. How the hummingbird spent that second is a mystery to me; perhaps it sipped nectar from the purple salvia in front of our door.

Goldfish the size of dinner plates are multiplying like bunnies. The goldfish keep their secrets. They do not gossip and they do not show their cards. They are poker faced, unlike the bunnies who pretty much let it all hang out all the time. You can always tell what a bunny is thinking, but goldfish are inscrutable. Even at dinner, they say little. They sit serenely with their fins undulating, gills bellowing. They seem attentive, but are not much for small talk.

WILDFIRES

Olga García Echeverría

I.
Bam! Just like that.
Another woman of color
eradicated by the system.
Why not start a wildfire
with all the newspaper articles?
It makes as much sense
as anything.

II.
She needed
more hummingbirds
more salvia
more seconds on the Universal clock

She needed
more nectar to sip
more time
to let it all hang out
to sit serenely, thinking
to small talk at dinner
to gossip with friends
She needed more time
to write
to birth
to live

to sleep
inside the safest place, her own navel,
spinning wheels of energy, yellow
Chakra vibrating, the mystery
of the undulating Universe
dripping from her fingertips

She needed more softness,
this purple-colored woman
bellowing through time,
wildfires in her eyes...

MY MILKY BLUES

Terry Wolverton

An atheist, a dolphin and a homo
walk into Heaven. God looks up but cannot
decipher their cratered faces. Rose water
spills onto the altar silk, marking it pink.

Long-stemmed and small-boned, I scatter whenever
rain spills against the church boat, unanchored in
a chalky sea. Amethyst breath of the moon
touches my face, baffles the infinite word.

You are native to the fierce depths, I am wrapped
in guns and dirty laundry. When we fuck we
go to Paradise, minus the amber ghosts.
All that upward leaping is just like marriage.

I keep imagining you're sad, translucent
mouth, a haiku in space with no gravity.
Those plush goodbyes made me gasp with poetry,
La Luna pillowed on the surface of time.

Sharks are now people. Women are pagan. Earth
is littered with injury. Heaven spotted
with scientists, armed with examples. God knows
who is the dead, red jelly in the charred heart.

READER POEM: A FARMWORKER OFFERS ADVICE TO A HUMMINGBIRD FLYING AMONG THE GRAPEVINES

Manuel J. Velez

Never let them count the thrusts of your wings;
the subtle motions that stir in their minds
images of nightgowns floating across ballroom floors.

They'll never see how each thrust tears away
at your body and weakens your soul.

Never let them see past your rainbow plumes;
the playful dance of colors that remind them
of exotic pearls resting softly around their necks.

They don't see that underneath the rainbow
lies the cold grey reality of a life spent at work.

Never let them measure the rhythm of your beating heart;
The soft vibrations that sing to them like a silent lullaby,
a serene moment of meditation.

They'll never know that each beat is a growing
desperation for survival.

No, hummingbird, never let them see who you truly are;

A creature trapped in the monotony of labor.
A perpetual existence of constant movement.
A life whose dream is for only enough nectar
to survive another day.

Let them be mesmerized by your motions.
Let them be captivated by your colors.
Let them believe that your true beauty is to be free.
Let them value that which least defines you
because it's the only way they'll find any value in you at all.

Manuel J. Velez received his MFA in Creative Writing from the University of Texas at El Paso's Bilingual Writing Program in 1996. Since then, aside from pursuing his literary goals, he has worked as a high school counselor and Spanish teacher in San Diego, an English Professor at El Paso Community College in El Paso, Texas and is currently Associate Professor of Chicana/o Studies at Mesa College. Manuel's work has appeared in various publications including *Raza Spoken Here Vol. 1, Many Mountains Moving,* and *Puerto del Sol.* He is the winner of the 1996 Pellicer-Frost Binational Poetry Prize and the author of *Bus Stops and Other Poems,* published by Calaca Press in 1998. Calaca Press also published *La Calaca Review,* an anthology of Latina/o voices edited by Manuel. He is currently chair of Chicana/o Studies at San Diego Mesa College.

Collaborating Poet: Sesshu Foster

Sesshu Foster has taught in East L.A. for 30 years. He's also taught writing at the University of Iowa, the California Institute for the Arts, Naropa University's Jack Kerouac School of Disembodied Poetics and the University of California, Santa Cruz. His work has been published in *The Oxford Anthology of Modern American Poetry, Language for a New Century: Poetry from the Middle East, Asia and Beyond,* and *State of the Union: 50 Political Poems.* Winner of two American Book Awards, his most recent books are the novel *Atomik Aztex* and the hybrid *World Ball Notebook.*

August Poetry PromptPoetry

Prompts from Sesshu Foster

- **CA Conrad (Soma)tic Poetry prompt:** Pick any (soma)tic poetry prompt by CA, this was one I could find at http://www.poets.org /poetsorg/poem/confetti-allegiance-love-letter-jim-brodey:

Confetti Allegiance

Is there a deceased poet who was alive in your lifetime but you never met, and you wish you had met? A poet you would LOVE to correspond with, but it's too late? Take notes about this missed opportunity. What is your favorite poem by this poet? Write it on unlined paper by hand (no typing). If we were gods we wouldn't need to invent beautiful poems, and that's why our lives are more interesting, and that's why the gods are always meddling in our affairs out of boredom. It's like the fascination the rich have with the poor, as Alice Notley says, "the poor are more interesting than others, almost uniformly." This poem was written by a human poet, and we humans love our poets, if we have any sense. Does something strike flint in you from the process of engaging your body to write this poem you know and love? Notes, notes, take notes.

The poet for me in doing this exercise is Jim Brodey and his poem "Little Light," which he wrote in the bathtub while listening to the music of Eric Dolphy, masturbating in the middle of the poem, "while the soot-tinted noise of too-full streets echoes / and I pick up the quietly diminishing soap & do / myself again." Take your handwritten version of the poem and cut it into tiny confetti. Heat olive oil in a frying pan and toss the confetti poem in. Add garlic, onion, parsnip, whatever you want, pepper it, salt it, serve it over noodles or rice. Eat the delicious poem with a nice glass of red wine, pausing to read it out loud and toast the poet, "MANY APOLOGIES FOR NOT TOASTING YOU WHEN YOU WERE ALIVE!" Take notes while slowly chewing the poem. Chew slowly so your saliva breaks the poem down before it slides into your belly to feed your blood and cells of your body. Gather your notes, write your poem.

• **a prompt from Bernadette Mayer's famous list:**
Write what cannot be written; for example, compose an index. http:// writing.upenn.edu/library/MayerBernadette_Experiments.html

• **a scientific one: Greatest Scientist of All Time**
Role: you; Audience: scientist from a past era; Format: written interview; Topic: the greatest contribution to science; Strong Verb: write and document

You have the opportunity to travel in a time machine into any past era of history. Choose a date and place to meet the person who, in your opinion, has made the greatest contribution to science. Write out the interview questions you will ask this scientist and document his or her answers. You will publish your interview when you return to the present. http://www.creative-writing-ideas-and-activities.com /science-writing-prompts.html

• **any prompt from jerome rothenberg's Technician's of the Sacred:**
(here's one): Looking for a way to spark your writing with imagery? Here's a great suggestion from Sheila Bender. Though the exercise is taken from her book *Writing Personal Poetry*, any writer can put it to use. Bender writes:

Recently I was standing on a hillside I had looked at years ago from a window at a writers conference. At that conference, I learned a useful exercise from my teacher Robert Hass, who went on to become the United States poet laureate. At the time, he was studying various culture's poetry using a book called Technicians of the Sacred. In Africa, he taught us, a tribe called the Bantu has an oral poetic tradition they exercise while working. One person says a line and, in the rhythm of the work, another answers with an association that shows the likeness between two objects or perceptions. "An elephant's tusk cracking" could get the response, "The voice of an angry man." That day, I looked at the hillside, saw wind in the grass and wrote, "Wind through the grass," and answered with the line, "I have the feeling you have written." Here are two-line bantus that students of mine have written in response to this exercise:

Write your own bantus, as many as you can. Try to evoke experiences of sound, taste and smell as well as touch and sight. This exercise is very much like metaphor and simile, but you are free of the need to make images grammatically correct and the results can be haunting. http:// www.writersdigest.com/writing-articles/by-writing-genre/horror-by-writing-genre/how_to_create_haunting_imagery.

Poetry Prompts from Terry Wolverton
• Hell's Zip Code
• Dreams Worth More than Money
• Slavery to Vegetables
• "I'm No Longer Afraid"

Fevered Writing by Sesshu Foster

Hell's Zip Code

Guadalupe to Union Station 7 pm great
white cumulus roiling cumulus upon cumulus
my little money tree
the student gave me, thanks! the idea that hell
hath a furious zip code: Kafkaesque letter carriers
scurrying to deliver dead letters
to some long dead forgotten LOS ANGELES
(Terminal Annex, of course) (of course)
open 24 hours like the gas station where the
woman set herself on fire, "I can't take this shit anymore"
image that light—seen from a great distance—a burning
human (Ana Mendieta) like L.A. on fire 1992,
prelude to Katrina

Dreams Worth More Than Money

San Gabriels sleeping, yucca, creosote, Spanish broom, tobacco
sleeping, decayed granite asleep and clouds of dreams in the arroyos,
over the canyons, pitted, rugged, desiccated ravines of
consciousness that resists (therefore coupled to) Eurocentric
"thinkers" (Beaudrillard, Benjamin, Semiotexte, whatever)
resistance within parameters of colonization, the
resistance of colonizers against mestizaje, dark bodies,
the dreams of the Other, the Othering of dreams,
"to suggestion the European variant is lonely thinking
of sole thoughts

Slavery to Vegetables

Upstate NY's blue mountains, they served us very (very)
nice home-made breads, scrumptious soups with barley in it,
like I said to somebody, "white people's food," but good!
Butter on fresh-baked breads, where do you get that?
I got a ticket driving south from the place on the wooded
highway— speeding, pulled over by female HP, "expired
registration," it wasn't my car! (I was to leave the vehicle
parked in the parking lot of the train station or airport,
whatever it was— its like a dream, faded ticket of a dream.)
Damp asphalt covered in leaves. Night flight across the
continent.

I'm No Longer Afraid

Mostly, they won't try to kill you, mostly, the dead dog will not
lift its head to speak, you will not long wander through vacuous
spaces of warehouse-like Mexico City market places seeking the
exit and your people, Koreatown on a busy afternoon, the Metro
line station at Western, Jose Lozano people surrounding you,
"in a flood of humanity," (black and white orchestral tones rising,
Charlie Chaplin's clock flits by like a barracuda in the strait) any
minute now I gotta go, I'll awaken, dispel the thin visions of poofy
memory, attendant sentiment and electric fan— Kerouac's notion,
"we're already dead," the male apocalyptic self-indulgence of
themselves as apotheosis, not the woman attending to business,
doing the chores. No longer afraid.

Fevered Writing by Terry Wolverton

Deceased poet: When the dead poets come to dinner I cover the floor in peanut shells. I lock the cat in the bedroom because someone is certain to be allergic. I serve similes as hors d'oeuvres and the glasses of absinthe glint green in the fading twilight. I can't seat a formalist next to a symbolist, or the LANGUAGE poets next to anyone. Everyone appreciates the strict meter of the main dish, but I find Whitman poking around in my kitchen cabinets, looking for the table salt.

What cannot be written are the names of all the dead, the ones disappeared, buried in mass graves, those who entered the prison and never came out, who swung from trees, were dragged behind cars, raped and raped by so many men until nothing was left. And the ones who mourn them, search for them, who travel to the capitol demanding answers, the ones who offer prayers, the ones who die themselves, never knowing. These names would set the page aflame, and burn down the world.

You are a medical scientist. You have devoted your life to a search for answers. You believe there are answers. You have placed your faith in reason, in the intellect, in progress. You are convinced that once answers are found, life will improve. Some days you find yourself just enamored with the idea of being the one to find the answers, you and nobody else. Some days you practice your acceptance speech for the Nobel Prize in the bathroom mirror before heading out to the lab. You believe anything is okay in pursuit of answers.

Wire hangars on a bar in the closet. They're like a group of men jostling elbows at a bar. The baseball game is on TV and the announcer's voice reminds you of childhood. The beer in front of you is sweating in its glass and the darkness heals the pain of the outside world—everyone rushing somewhere, doing things they imagine are important but which really mean nothing in the press of time. You order a hot pastrami sandwich, douse it in mustard, grab a handful of peanuts in the shell and let them crack in your giant hand.

FOR TERRY WOLVERTON

Sesshu Foster

burn down the world, because the beer in front of you sweats in its glass
because of a hot pastrami sandwich, pastrami with mustard
because of the glasses, the cars, everyone rushing somewhere
because of a TV and the announcer's voice
because of the cat locked in the bedroom, because of anything, because of
    the trees
because of so many in cars rushing in fading twilight, enamored of darkness
burn down the world,
burn down the world

outside the world, everyone is okay, doing things they imagine
outside of the world, you dragged your intellect to mass graves and prison
outside of the world, anything is prayer, nobody practices at childhood
outside the world, those who entered the glinting pain and came out
outside the trees, those who entered the green, you and nobody else
outside the world, those who entered the trees and disappeared
outside the world, you and nobody else
in front of you, you and nobody else

I cover the floor in salt,
there you will find yourself
next to anyone, next to many men who die themselves
I cover the floor in fading twilight,
there you will find yourself
like a crack in your hand, because you are convinced,
because you are certain, next to poets and many who answer the press of time
I cover the floor in similes,
like similes of wire and reason, there you will find yourself
next to the TV of childhood and the announcer's voice
let these reasons remind you of a handful of names,
a handful of days

HELL'S ZIP CODE

Terry Wolverton

A letter carrier in Koreatown
dreams of women, bodies dark as tobacco
dreams of resistance, of granite and flood.

The hour is apocalyptic.
Money and fire are killing us.

Union Station decaying, no train of thoughts
will leave this afternoon, no great distance will
be covered, now the terminal is burning.

We sought a damp, vacuous sleep.
We awakened to slavery.

In Mexico City, NY, LA— we're
rolling through markets of the colonizers
surrounded by dead, Eurocentric thinkers.

Where do we exit this head space?
Where is the clock forgotten?

Across this continent females and males no
longer couple, busy themselves annexing
the lonely minutes, but there's no where to park.

We no longer see the other
across canyons of sentiment.

Spanish broom rises over the mountains, but
we can't drive there anymore, no vehicle,
no gas. No place not covered in black asphalt.

What is your vision worth to you,
already dispelling in clouds?

It's the cumulus that leaves me furious.
Is this a prelude to light, or are we like
the thin dogs that wander the pitted highway?

We flit within parameters;
got a ticket but can't take flight.

The letter carrier will not open this
hand-made letter to herself, delivered in
blue notes from her faded memory, her dreams.

READER POEM: INVITATION TO CA CONRAD

Henry Medina

Let's say the obvious
so our lives
resemble art

In the crucible of our being
let's create
gods
and stories

Let's create nothing
better
let
the things emerge
damp from our souls

Let's tell our hearts
to unlearn fear
to recount yesterday
accurately

Let's be
little rivers of water
crumbling
the defects of our lives

Let's change something
so its wave of effects
will lift us
tomorrow

Let's wash
away with the present

Let's
find the ending first
before the beginning

Henry Medina received his BA in English from Cornell University. When he is not writing for fun, he is playing with his chickens, bunnies and piglets on his farm. He is currently writing his first book, a collection of short stories.

Collaborating Poet: Donna Frazier

Donna Frazier: Realized early that poetry is an oasis for a nonlinear mind flying about in a linear world. Fell in love with it. Spent time with great teachers like William Matthews, Marie Ponsot and Terry Wolverton. Is always writing and editing, much of the time for other people, but in the best moments for her own muses. Has published work in places like *Mudlark* and *First Things*. A collection of her dreamy and practical inspiration for writers is on her website at: www.donnafrazier.com/news.

Editor's Note: Donna and Terry were each invited to create original poems for the "Oasis" exhibition at Descanso Gardens. They decided to use their dis•articulations collaboration to generate those poems. They found their prompts on the grounds at Descanso (interptetive signage, promotions brochures, book titles in the bookstore, and even a chance encounter with another visitor), and did their fevered writing on-site. Their poems were exhbited in the natural landscape of the gardens from September to December of 2015.

September Poetry Prompts

Poetry Prompts from Donna Frazier

• Babies may dangle temporarily

• Reflected light, right-side up

• Hooker's manzanita (Arctostaphylus hookeri, "wayside")

• "Not by works of law" (Text from a garden visitor's Bible. Walking near the Haaga Gallery, I spotted a man carrying something under his arm that might be a journal, might be a book.

Exchange:

"Excuse me, is that a book you're carrying?"

"Yes, it's the Bible."

"Would you mind opening it and turning to a random page?"

[Pulls book from under his arm and starts to open it.]

"Are you seeking guidance?"

"No, it's for a project. So could you pick a random passage?"

"How about a NOT random passage? [turns with some intent to the back of the Bible.]

I glance at the pages he's opened to and let my eyes focus on something. "Not by works of law" is what comes to the surface.

Poetry Prompts from Terry Wolverton:

• Cowboy cologne

• Deer are particularly fond of roses

• Garden Dancer Cha Cha

• Extreme Snakes Tattoos

Fevered Writing by Donna Frazier

Cowboy cologne … smells like what I imagine cactus smells like, dust and point, odd unanticipated flower just stuck there on the end of a paddle. I don't know how they apply it, the flower or the scent, but you can feel it coming like some cedar path you weren't expecting on the side of the street you've lived on for so many years you've stopped seeing it or the forest at its edge, saplings when you moved in. Birds are circling the trunks like lunberjacks or cowboys in that flow of herd, the river of it that they lasso and tie up.

Deer are particularly fond of roses. It's the petals, which fall from the mouth like tongues, speech flying to the ground, unexpected thought. They eat alone, the deer in the rose garden, the colors tender, the sounds crunching in the mouth. I can't understand the dialect of rose they speak, but they look up as I pass and I drop leaves, a conversation we leave on the trail behind us. I had tasted the buds myself but found them tough. No allergies though. Later I dreamed of clover and running.

Garden dancer cha-cha. I say they oughta waltz or stand still, but I know I'm wrong. They've planted snow peas and asparagus and the music is some kind of fertilizer, the dance a kind of vibration therapy. Okay. I could give in to a little swing, a little something shaking the shoots and my hair taking on a little green in solidarity, the shoots sprouting from fingers that might or might not be mine. In the shade, the dance slows to a single cha, but the plants anticipate the beats and keep on moving.

Extreme snake tattoo. I don't know why the snakes need them. Diamonds, stripes, that "blend with sand" pattern, seem like enough. But some want more, like the red flashes on the side of a turtle's head, that kind of bling. Snakes on the arms and legs of a human? They hang from limbs waiting for prey I guess, trying to blend in. Inside the skins, reptilian and otherwise, there's ink flowing, needles and buzz, some identity exchanged.

Fevered Writing by Terry Wolverton

Baby may dangle temporarily but sooner or later they float up into the air and hover over the city in their brightly colored layettes like balloons accidentally loosed by a careless child. The babies are unafraid, being so high in the sky; they like having a view of everything—the tops of trees and the puffy clouds and the roofs of homes and the flag poles at the school they will never have to go to now. They speak with the birds and they speak to God. You can hear them crooning their little songs.

Hooker's Manzanita It has a bad reputation, but don't judge. You don't know what you would do if you were hungry or had gotten kicked out of the house or were addicted to drugs you had no money to buy. Why a hook, I always wonder? Is it because they supposedly lure you in? If anything, these women seem like the ones who are hooked, like fish once free in the river, then dangling by the mouth and bleeding. She liked to do it underneath the trees, the big old trees with spreading leaves.

Not by works of law because living things are subject to our own laws, directions of destiny and the expanse of spirit. You cannot pin us down or confine us to certain rooms or make us do things we don't want to do. You can try, and you do try, and you have courts and police and judges and jails and armies but still you are unable to change the course of nature. The river will overflow its banks despite the concrete and the lover will do the hurtful thing despite promises and no matter how you press, we will escape.

Reflective light right side up. It's said that Narcissus stared into the surface of the pool and glimpsed his own image. He lived in a time without mirrors and he thought it was another man he saw—a beautiful young man. He could not do anything then but spend his days gazing into the water, yearning for his object of desire, who always left him at night. How the moon teased him, giving him the merest suggestion of his beloved, shadowy and uncertain. Only the sun was faithful.

WHAT THE TREES KNOW

Donna Frazier

Once you were bird float and tree song,
cloud mouth pressed to sky, no desire

but light. You were spirit teased from
time and its beautiful hooks, matter

loosed and crooning in the mirrored
night. It's said we were kicked out,

bleeding into cities, jailed and judged
without wonder. But beloved,

I have glimpsed you gazing into
narcissus and manzanita,

changed by the thought of escape.
You home to the big old trees,

giving yourself over to God and his
armies of leaves, to birds spreading

down layettes on the concrete banks
of rivers. Our nature is to want,

to try, to balloon into yearning,
but beloved, be still, be faithful

only to now. You are moon and air
and lover. Freed, you are only expanse.

BEHIND THE GARDEN

Terry Wolverton

You, cowboy, did not dream the trail—
needles of red dust circling
in unexpected dialect,
cha-cha of the diamond streets.

I shook a river from my hair;
it still flowed the color of ink.
Tattoos sprouted on my legs — deer
striping a path, shade of cedar.

The conversation was extreme—
not human, but something tender
falling from the tongues of roses,
unanticipated music.

Mouth of cactus, forest of prey.
Why does the turtle try to fly?
Fingers the color of saplings,
we waltz on a green edge alone.

The vibrational speech of skin
cannot be slowed or stopped, sounds like
a lasso tying me to a
swing, odd crunch of leaves as I drop.

READER POEM: PLACEMENT

Trista Hurley-Waxali

Before he'd say,
the nectar was too sweet for him to enjoy.
But that changed after Samantha left.

Seasons came and went as he'd roam,
leaving her to nest in their range of land.
Rumor was that she never got over her first love—
the buck who lost,
that she'd walk the border, hoping to pick-up
his scent.

So when Carl came home that night
and saw his doe was no longer there,
we all knew where she went.

We watch him now, grieving the loss,
unsure of her death,
unsure of her life.
Moving the petals with his cloven hoof
trying to frame the floor-bed
they once shared.

Trista Hurley-Waxali is the author of the poetry chapbook *Dried Up*. Her work has appeared in *FORTH, Enclave,* and *Street Line Critics*, and in the *Procyon Short Story Anthology 2014*. She has performed at the O'bheal Poetry Series in Cork, Ireland and in a Helsinki Poetry Connection Poetry Jam TransLate Night Show. Trista is working on her first novel, *At This Juncture*.

Collaborating Poet: Ramón García

october

Ramón García is author of *The Chronicles* (Red Hen Press, 2015), *Other Countries* (What Books Press, 2010) and *Ricardo Valverde* (University of Minnesota Press, 2013), He has published poetry in a variety of journals and anthologies including *Best American Poetry 1996, Ambit, The Floating Borderlands: Twenty-Five Years of US-Hispanic Literature, Crab Orchard Review, Poetry Salzburg Review, Los Angeles Review*, and *Mandorla: New Writing from the Americas*. A founding member of the Glass Table Collective, an artist collective formed in 2008, he is a professor at California State University, Northridge and lives in Los Angeles.

October Poetry Prompts

Poetry Prompts from Ramón García

- ...no one can be slain in absentia or in effigie.
- These first three Steps are the acceptance Steps.
- Narcissus, the solitary, is the very image of the adolescent.
- Bloom is aware of conspicuous omissions...

Poetry Prompts from Terry Wolverton

- Don't say his name
- I never thought Michiko would come back
  after she died.
- Einstein ring helps weigh a black hole
- "Live from the Gutter"

Fevered Writing by Ramón García

Don't say his name

Don't say his name, say his mask.

Say his other name, the one that is not him, the name that is her.

Don't say his name, say his face, his thousand faces.

Say what is not his name, his other name.

Don't say what is not his name, say what is.

Don't say his name, say Gertrude Stein.

Say this and say that but don't say I didn't tell you his name.

Say this name not that name, say it's his and not a name.

Say all names and say his, but don't say his name.

Say all that is his, his name and his not name.

Say his name, but don't.

Say it, say his name and not his name, his mask and his face.

I never thought Michiko would come back after she died.

I never thought Michiko would come back after she did. But why not? People die and people come back. They're called ghosts. They are called Michiko. To come back one must be dead, but who said so? Maybe Michiko said so, that's why she died and came back as a ghost. Or maybe it was not a ghost just someone who comes back. After death, maybe it's all a coming back to something. To a something called Michiko. I like the sound of the name and therefore it's ghostly, beyond life, which is rhythm, which is language.

Einstein ring helps weigh a black hole

Einstein ring helps weigh a black what? A black hole. A black hole in the wall. A black ring? What is an Einstein ring? Don't' ask me because I don't know. I only know that it's black and it's a whole cause that's what the saying says, that's what the Earthsky says. What I say when I say what I write. This sounds like Einstein on the Beach, and it might be. But what beach, what Einstein, what sky? Why? Why sky? Why Einstein, which Einstein?

Live from the Gutter

Live from my Gutter. Live from what Gutter? Is Gutter a place, a geography? Or is it a state of being? Can it be a state of being, a Gutter. Can it be the name of a person or a cat? Gutter. It has a name ring to it. It has a song written into it. It has something to ring a song into it's Gutter. Into it, it's something and it's alive. It's alive to what is gutter. To what is guttering. To what is a song and what is Gutter. Guttersnipe. What is a guttersnipe? I really don't know. Is it a song? An unknown song, and is Gutter the root word of a gutter word? I don't know. It's a song. Let it be in the gutter, without capitalizing a gutter, a Gutter. It's alive, it's live and black and it's a hole. It's a sky and it's a Gutter. Help.

Fevered Writing by Terry Wolverton

No on can be slain in absentia or in effigie. I disagree. The night is long and one can die a thousand deaths at the hands of others' imaginations. How they slaughter me--those who believe I have wronged them and those who envy something in my house, those who dispute my politics and those who have an ancient feud with my ancestors. All night long, I stagger and fall, rise again only to succumb to poison or bullets, fire or gossip. I am slain.

These first three steps are the acceptance steps. The recovery cha-cha is a new dance craze but I am tripping over my feet again, stumbling across the floor, looking for my partner who is passed out on the bandstand. Her vomit cakes my new shoes, but still I make the moves— one-two-three and one-two-three, and my nose is shiny with the effort and no one is looking at me. I used to love to dance, a little girl in a tutu and everyone would smile but those days are over and now the music sounds like a machine that's breaking.

Narcissus, the solitary, is the very image of the adolescent. Why would they make it take so long before our brains develop? Why would someone engineer a being who was capable of reproducing long before its brain could make a good decision? Has something gone haywire with the food we eat or the water we drink or the chemicals we ingest? Are we developmentally delayed? Maybe we need to remain solitary until our brain catches up to our hormones.

Bloom is aware of conspicuous omissions. What is the awareness of a bloom? Science tells us plants sense when another plant is in trouble and they send out shoots in that plant's direction. They try to help. This means plants are sentient, another blow to our pathetic theories of superiority. Plants will be around to clean up the mess after we blow it all up.

FOUR POEMS

Ramón García

The night can die
       A thousand deaths
Other's slaughter   who believe
House   dispute
       Ancient feud—ancestor night
Stagger, rise, succumb
       To fire or gossip

       Slain
      ***

Recovery craze tripping
       Stumbling
My partner   out
       Bandstand vomit
       Shoes make moves
Shiny looking   love tutu

Smile   over music breaking
      ***

Make it   brain engineer
Being brain
       Haywire food
Ingest delayed
Remain solitary brain
       Up to our hormones

      ***

Awareness of Bloom
Plants sense
Another plant in trouble
Shoots in the plant's direction
          Help
Sentient blow   pathetic theories
          Superiority
Around the mess
                    Blow

CALLING YOU BACK

Terry Wolverton

Gertrude Stein comes back from the dead
to ask what it is like without you.
Is she the ghost, or is it me?
Words ring out from the black sky
of her face, sound like a song
telling the geography of death,
a place beyond the thousand walls.

Einstein comes back with a black cat;
I ask him its name. He says
her name is Michiko and she comes
from the gutters of the after life.
Her language is unknown to some
but when I sound out the rhythms,
I know she is calling for help.

Without you I am without the root.
The beach is ghostly. There's a hole
in the sky that weighs on me.
People say let her be, but I cannot.
Beyond the mask I have no face,
only the songs I will never write.
Of all the names, I call just one.

READER POEM: WHEN YOU CALL FOR THE DEAD
DON'T SAY HIS NAME

Liz Belile

A father curled up in bed
skinny as a hound or
Christ on the cross

A boy in full flower
head thrown back laugh
knuckles green with morning glory

I wake up in sweat
I turn like a cyclone in my too-small sheets
the phone vibrates
I don't know the number
so I pick up & pray
Don't say his name

The bullet dodged
the ship I grazed
while at sea
the one who got away
with it
when I thought
the chamber was hollow
buried me in a shallow rut
that one
Don't say his name

There is a god
so dark and unknown
unwilling to enunciate he drowns us all
in his muck
Don't say his name

When they fuck
and all she can think of is
the piercing blue
or the wolf scent
of the other
Don't say his name

You can call me
tumble me in your open air
but when it all comes down

and the awards are handed over
Don't say his name

Liz Belile studied poetry at the Naropa Institute and her work has been published widely. She lives in Austin, Texas with her family, where she teaches screenwriting at a local film school and occasionally produces poetry readings and teaches yoga, among other subversive activities.

Collaborating Poet — Douglas Kearney

Eric Plattner

november

Douglas Kearney's third poetry collection, *Patter* (Red Hen Press, 2014) examines miscarriage, infertility, and parenthood and was a finalist for the California Book Award in Poetry. Cultural critic Greg Tate remarked that Kearney's second book, National Poetry Series selection, *The Black Automaton* (Fence Books, 2009), "flows from a consideration of urban speech, negro spontaneity and book learning." A collection of opera libretti—*Some-one Took They Tongues*—is forthcoming from Subito Press. Noemi Press will publish his collection of writing on poetics and performativity—*Mess and Mess and* in late 2015. He has received a Whiting Writer's Award, residencies/fellowships from Cave Canem, The Rauschenberg Foundation, and others. His work has appeared in a number of journals, including *Poetry, nocturnes, Pleiades, Iowa Review, Boston Review,* and *Callaloo;* and anthologies including *Best American Poetry, Best American Experimental Writing, Wide Awake,* and *What I Say: Innovative Poetry by Black Poets in America.* Raised in Altadena, CA, he lives with his family in California's Santa Clarita Valley. He teaches at CalArts.

November Poetry Prompts

Poetry Prompts from Douglas Kearney
- "crisco fried funk"
- "only a partial relationship to reality"
- "vulgar yet weirdly graceful"
- "the infantilization of people of color and women"

Poetry Prompts from Terry Wolverton
- Hard Day of the Dead Dances on
- Why Latinos Love Horror Films
- Montage of Heck
- Robot doctors and lawyers

Fevered Writing by Douglas Kearney

Hard Day of the Dead Dances on

come on everybody got a day of the zombie get down to the boogey-
man up jump the spooky to the end of time I saw what you done
did with the cold pulse and then the strobelit honey to the similac. a
pepper tree, naw naw naw, but you climbed and chucked down on
some kinkajou mojo. It wasn't a primate but it dilated. any way the
skeleton oh and find the bones find the bones. the goofer dust is the
do it fluid, the kambucha of your hoodoo fix. we be talking all kinds
of roots. the alex haley to the two head I can't tell you how many times
I've tried to paint bones on a suit only to find I could just trace my
own cage.

Why Latinos Love Horror Films

because of love and the old time religion that goes back further how
edith Hamilton oh dear frosty edith tried to side eye anypeople who
could imagine god's powerful enough to not look like them all day.
egomaniacs! the bottom line is a thought of blodd that ain't always
limpieza, but I wonder that too. thinking of Lorca and the blood shot
through his deep song and anytime you think latinos why you gotta
trot out Lorca. but Soul is Duende in a sketch but not janky only quick
like and del toro (red cape as blood is red) as a vampire is a robot insect
as U.S. looks down, breathing red eyed from its attic

Montage of Heck

heck of a job heck of a thing to say heck of a heckler of a jeckle them magpies oh Terry(toons) I'm in love! the fact of the matter is Cobain I see all in that weird fleece flapped cap looking all, well, fucking Cobainesque. we can be disappointed in a choice right but hell what would you do with them barrels looking you in the face like those times you climb something high and have to tell yourself "don't jump. don't jump" like how to not ogle you say "don't look. don't look." or when you are impatient with Nicole you say "don't say _____. don't say _____."

Robot doctors and lawyers

Doctors for robots and lawyers for them or doctors and lawyer robots? Litigibot. Docbot. The kind of machine that knows how to find precedent. I would get an attorneybot a botister, a cyberadvocate, oh shit, like how Lety saw "mecha Godzilla" and thought it was like a chicano kaiju. I don't know about what kind of curative a robot would need to take and I don't have time for any more puns but I could imagine how the robot would enter on it's conveyer, a special appendage for cupping testicles, a speaker grill buzzing *cough* cough* cough*

Fevered Writing by Terry Wolverton

Crisco fried funk

I think of Crisco, white and bland in the can, its impassive face revealing nothing. Likely it has no thoughts, but heat it up and its complexion clears and it starts hopping in the pan, popping on the stove, splattering a little sting onto the cook's unsuspecting skin. Drop in the funk, itself just an unformed wad of dough, and watch it begin to spin and brown and harden somehow, growing a toasty coat on the outside and a soft cake inside.

Only a partial relationship to reality

The philosopher said, "reality is agreement," so I said goodbye to reality a long time ago. Once you cut yourself loose, there's no turning back. You can't even imagine how you got bamboozled into it in the first place. The imagination has no place in reality--it's all about "what it is" rather than what it could be. Living in possibility requires adaptation to a cooler kind of light, a thinner oxygen. Your survival is not guaranteed. But you begin to love that edge, the tipsiness of every day.

Vulgar yet weirdly graceful

People have a lot of contempt for this kind of woman. They want her to be more like a butterfly, less like a baboon. They want her to wear little slips of dresses and not get her hands dirty, to tiptoe about on the thinnest heels, not to ground her soles into Mother Earth. They want her to pretend she has no body, that her body belongs to them and she may not enjoy it. She's not supposed to acknowledge her slash, her gash, her split in the universe through which light enters.

The infantilization of people of color and women, and the women who are people of color are the most babied of all, but not babied in the Western post-industrial middle class model of doting and spoiling and commodifying, no, more like the pre-capitalist model of property, like livestock. Like infanticide. No one is dressing us up in doll clothes and fussing over us. No, we are dragged by the hair and beaten until our cries no longer disturb their sleep. Who's your daddy, they ask, but we've learned better than to answer, our mouths sewn shut, our tongues snipped out.

THE LIVESTOCK

Douglas Kearney

we've places in our properties for them,
lots for growing them into lots more for us.
in the places, there, we can watch them,
our faces like hands having want. we, beaten

by a cooler outside, said they got a coat kind-of-
a-skin sewn up on their body until—beaten
by the cooler outside—we slip them out it
to wear it on us and so we

are we, for we wear their skin for us.

by our stove-like imagination,
in it, they are a wad of living Crisco,
Crisco shut up in them until we cook it
out them, them out it, into a pan, a cut of them
fried in it out a can and into our mouths,
ground inside our mouths turning us into we-
who-wear-wads-of-body-in-our-bodies
and the wad's bodies on our bodies and so we

are we, for we cook to enjoy this insiding.

times, we've agreements with us
to think for them impassive bodies what they think
our love is like, so we spin answers out slashed mouths,

snipped tongues, the splatterings beaten out their they
in our lots for growing us out of them:

we say they may say we are universes gashing Earth

or baboons long ago hardened into clothes

or that by their brown livings we guarantee us
they want in our mouths, to be our coats,
to tiptoe their they through our imaginations,
graceful as, doting as mothers sewn to cries.

no no no no no—our love is nothing but goodbye.
and how we only want to love it all and so

all of them.

JANKY MOJO

Terry Wolverton

I came in with janky mojo,
head peppered with hard thoughts,
face painted with Kaiju's blood,
skeleton in a spooky suit.

Who was that vampire in a red cape,
its song tracing through my pulse,
heckling my impatient choices,
talking shit about God?

When did I become a cold machine
that breathes frost and coughs dust?
My bone cage jumps
in the attic of my disappointment.

Lorca too was disappointed
in the magpie's quick-like song.
My appendages cannot climb
to any honey pulse to fix it.

But egomaniacs love religion,
think it's all about them.
Gods dance like insects in my head,
and cup my red-eyed soul.

End-times only a strobe-lit
boogeyman, just enough horror
that sometimes I look side-eye
through the flapping trees.

In the end, my fluid roots
the only curative to not bottom out.
I came in abuzz with janky mojo
and no hoodoo gonna take it back.

READER POEM: MONTAGE

Jennifer Hernandez

Huaraches across the borderlands or
dinghies on the open sea. Which shall
we choose, people of color -- infantilization
or demonization? Migrants. Refugees.
Illegals. Terrorists. The rhetoric bears only
a partial relationship to reality.
Swaddle us and stick a big old plug
in our mouths. Restraint and silence.

You want to know why Latinos
like horror films? Maybe
because we know that kind of scary
is fake. We got enough real. Los narcos.
La inmigrácion checking for papers.
Le deportaron a mi tío. His baby girl cries
herself to sleep. Hatemongers splash venom
like red paint. Why can't they see that the rapists
are the pinche coyotes that steal our money
and leave us in the desert?

So the Day of the Dead dances on.
Esquéletos draped in marigolds spin
clackety-clack before altars to the music of mariachi
and banda. If we stop dancing, we're already dead.

Jennifer Hernandez teaches immigrant youth, wrangles three sons and writes for her sanity. She lives in Minnesota with her husband and family, which also includes a black lab and a fat lap cat. She has recently performed her poetry as part of the Cracked Walnut Literary Festival and as honorable mention in the Elephant Rock flash prose contest. Her work appears in *Silver Birch Press* and *Talking Stick,* as well as other print and online journals.

Collaborating Poet: Yvonne M. Estrada

Yvonne M. Estrada is the author of the chapbook, *My Name on Top of Yours*, a crown of sonnets accompanied by original photographs. Her poems have recently appeared in *Talking Writing, Fourth & Main, Lit For Life* and in the anthologies, *Coiled Serpent: Poets Arising from the Cultural Quakes and Shifts of Los Angeles; Wide Awake: Poets of Los Angeles and Beyond; Like a Girl: Perspectives on Feminine Identity;* and *Gutters and Alleyways: Perspectives on Poverty and Struggle*, which also included one of her photographs.

December Poetry Prompts

Poetry Prompts from Yvonne M. Estrada:

- In very simple English they call it good luck.
- ...an exploration of the absurdity of our own existence
- We were lucky that our water tanks were filled before the electricity failed
- Slow and patient centuries can grow to create structures hundreds of miles long

Poetry Prompts from Terry Wolverton:

- Republicans are not the condom police
- Written on beasts
- Of being engine red
- When it's dark out

Fevered Writing by Yvonne M. Estrada

republicans are not the condom police but really they are they want to see what you're doing in the bedroom they want to make sure that there's a hole in every condom more women to control all the better their perverse enjoyment. their ancient relatives fucking sheep on a boat inventing venereal disease and beastiality simultaneously. they drive around in their little police cars pulling people over to see if they have their condoms on, they lie! they are the condom police! it's all their fault they are the Dickheadz of the millenium

written on beasts is the true creation story. the man made ones are so predictable. the words are tattooed by tapping a sharp stick dipped in ink from a net full of octopi pulled from the ocean and lugged back to the stortellers hut where the wild horses flinch but do not run away they must spread the word they know no one else will bother

of being engine red the fire starts of being sky blue because the wind can only be felt of being gold are our friends we knew before the age of computers of being brown there are those that will never know of being crushed until there is nothing left bit a good way to die

when it's dark out I play it in the ambrosial hours only. once the sun rises i no longer understand the words. at night there are so many people that can overhear. I need the cover of the dark so I can see what's going on without being detected. Under the radar I listen to albums by rap stars. under the stars I listen to G easy and his new album. when it's dark out I can breathe I can see I can feel the warmth coming up from the sidewalk of the day's sun. things are quieter the hush of traffic. children gone to bed.

Fevered Writing by Terry Wolverton

In very simple English they call it good luck, as if the heavens were smiling down upon you, clearing the path with a sweep of angel wings, divesting all obstacles and keeping you from harm—no traffic tickets, no dog bites, no scaly rashes, no overdue bills. Instead there are flowers and trees and fluffy clouds and your favorite songs always on the radio and the woman you love never disappoints you and everyone admires you for you poems.

An exploration of the absurdity of our existence. It's more like a recipe—two parts "Can you believe it?" to one part "What the fuck." Add a pinch of "God has a sick sense of humor." There might as well be laughter, pee-your-pants laughter, because otherwise it is all too unbearable. So put on the clown shoes and hop into the tiny car. Bend over and rip the back of your drawers. Squirt yourself with a bottle of seltzer. Be the one who laughs so you're not the one laughed at. In the end, it's just a pie in the face.

We were lucky that our water tanks were filled before the electricity failed. Because when the monsoons came they would have washed away the big screen TVs and the high tech exercise machines, but fortunately the earth had already swallowed them up in the big quake that triggered the meltdown at the nuclear plant. The cows were born sickly after that but we don't eat cows in my country, so the loss of human life was minimal. We are so lucky that we know we'll be reborn under better circumstances, that everything we see now is illusion.

Slow and patient centuries can grow to create structures hundreds of miles long. It's like our story, hundreds of miles of words and images and memory, our history, our language, our culture—all a construction. If I blink my eyes it is gone and I'm journeying to a new world where it all looks different and if there is sky, I will call it something else and maybe it's yellow instead of blue or maybe a color I can't perceive in this current structure. Or maybe it's music, or maybe I have no senses anymore but just know things via some other organ. Or maybe there is no "I" but just one energy.

HUMAN RECIPE STORY

Yvonne M. Estrada

Overdue laughter
triggered a high-tech
monsoon.

Everything was reborn
lucky, flowers yellow
and sky blue.

Fortunately,
angels' wings
sweep everything.

Centuries of memory
become paths
to heaven.

Miles and miles
of illusion
gone.

LISTEN

Terry Wolverton

I rise from the bed of words
where we fuck in perverse ink,
tattoo the sheets gold and blue.
Words are little boats
on an ocean of sheets.
We spread our nets, dip in,
but words run wild;
we can never control their play.

By day, we are only women,
beasts with holes covered up,
our creations policed,
crushed by the dickheads' sharp words,
flinching into the red sun.
Hush, they can overhear
our venereal warmth,
detect our ambrosial breath.

Around the fire at night,
we are children
writing on the sky,
tattooing horses in the dark.
I know the ancient stories
but you invented the stars.
Wherever we are,
it will never be quiet.

Listen. I will make a true hut
of words and never leave it.
You traffic in story,
tap it out on every sidewalk.
If it's a predictable disease,
it's not our fault.
It is the wind's sure breath
that bothers the golden hours.

READER POEM: ENGINE RED

Micki Blenkush

When the Master who cast us
tires of our absurd stage
will directions come forth
beyond the signs foretold?
Not just the seven horseman
or the white buffalo calf
but actual words written on beasts.
Skunks with caution striped
across their backs or fish with listen
stitched in their scales.

Any language can already predict
propaganda past meaning
even as wolves and panthers arrive
with grief spelled down their sides.
In simple English we'll call it luck
each time there's a storm
and all we have to worry about
is what to eat first
when the power goes out.
No one yet at our door
with a machine gun
tells us how to believe.

This is the red of emergency.
Of persons stalled in the turn lane
unsure what to do for the sirens.
This is the color of a woodpecker's head
persisting along the eaves
despite my banging at windows
and inspecting for holes.
This is the hue of a grandmother's voice
when she wept my name.
I never heard that color before,
but wanted to move everything back
to let it pass through.

Micki Blenkush works as a social worker in Minnesota and lives with her spouse and daughter. Her poetry has appeared in: *Sequestrum, Naugatak River Review, Heron Tree, Red Earth Review,* among other online and print publications.

REFLECTIONS ON THE PROCESS

At the conclusion of each month, Terry Wolverton invited the collaborating poet to offer comments on their experience of participating in the dis•articulations project.

January: Jessica Ceballos

It's easy to pull words from the same pool we allot ourselves, so what makes this project difficult, but equally rewarding, is that those words may not be in this pool of words. This forces us to look beyond the usual way we've trained our brains to respond to the themes that interest us. And that creates this domino effect of forcing us to look beyond those usual ideas or structures. I found myself taking notes while trying to figure out what the next line was gonna be, because some of the words whispered to me some pretty wild ideas. Also, I'm always looking for different processes, and using the fevered writings as thesaurus is my new favorite; it's constrictive, which I find helps me focus on an idea, while at the same time, not having the words might let us get away with writing somewhat abstractly. A really wonderful project. Thank you so much for inviting me Terry!

February: Mike Sonksen

I really enjoyed the process of dis•articulations. Over the years I have used both the collage method and cut-up technique for writing poems many times. This exercise reminded me of that. Some of the phrases from Terry's fevered writing were so poignant that I used them close to verbatim in different parts of my poem. I looked for aligning themes and also tried to de-familiarize the meaning by putting different clauses together in a different order. Some of the lines had words that were rearranged from Terry's word bank. Originally I composed a longer poem and then decided to cut some of it. I began by trying to use all of the words and came up with a poem that was close to 50 lines long. I then decided to trim about 7 or 8 lines to make it crisper. In many ways this exercise is comparable to putting together a puzzle. I enjoyed the challenge and would gladly do it again.

March: A.K. Toney

The dis•articulation form is one of the codes for creating poetry. As the prompt enters your critical thought process, the fevered writing becomes some other entity, the responses from the other writer you receive become an elaboration on that code for creating. This is a vice-versa process that allows one to examine someone other than themselves and pull resources for a poem. It allowed me to look at other writings from myself and jumpstart new ideas about poetry and form. Moreover, dis•articulation inspired me about the pedagogy of poetry.

April: Angela Peñaredondo

The fevered writing process felt somewhat awkward at first, like any creative endeavor starting from scratch. The ego spoke as usual, judging and critiquing, even at times timid and confused, but that only lasted a few seconds. Three minutes is not long, so I had to get over the self-critic fast. It's an interesting process when you let the mind open up to whatever washes in and out. It's almost like being submissive to the words, which was pretty cool!

This was one of my favorite poetic collaborations. I would do it again. Terry is awesome to work with; she knows this process and how to lead it. She follows through, which does not happen with all collaborative work. So I deeply respect and adore her for this.

Personally, I need deadlines. I can easily lose myself in the small details of anything, become distracted by other projects or acts/performances of mundanity. Deadlines can be pretty crucial to my creative process. They keep me in check like an alarm clock or a personal trainer. I thought the timeline for this project was perfect.

May: Chiwan Choi

Over the years, the one thing that I have never been able to prepare for while setting out on a writing project is the element of life, the surprises it brings upon you, the chaos/sadness/joy that comes unexpectedly. It affects the way I work, what I wanted to say, how much time I have to say it. And it was no different this time. While in the middle of this project, so many Life things occurred that took my time and energy and focus away. All these things are challenges in themselves, but having to write, to speak, with words dictated by someone else's prompt, then ultimately, use only a limited amount of words that have been given to you by someone else really frustrated me. Which led to the questions—What are words? Who do they belong to? What does it mean to be constrained? Do words equal privilege? Do words equal identity? And ultimately, who am I speaking for when we are assigning sequences to shared vocabulary?

June: Elena Karina Byrne

Terry Wolverton's inspiration is a tour de force. She embodies many of the reasons we become writers in the first place.

Her project dis•articulations 2015 was my first adventure (marvelous misadventure) into a guided automatic writing based on found non-poetry source materials. This process is proof the mind (conscious and unconscious) can reinvent language context—that context is a spacial orientation in the imagination, and language springs from each writer's emotional, historical archeology-place. Language and image resurrected asymmetrically. I found that the disengagement of new language and its confined structure of using all the available words actually created a lyrical freedom and overriding feeling of creative urgency. There was a kinetic propellant to the instantaneous daydreaming process forced within the compressed three-minute prompt time frame given. Poetry like this emerges vertically and, for me, is simply desire in motion.

July: Olga García Echeverría

This collaborative writing exercise was quite a journey. I liked that I didn't really know where I was going. Most challenging was the act of sitting with someone else's words and trying to inject my own poetic voice and vision into the disarticulated mix. I played a lot during the past couple of weeks and put together several drafts of different poems, but in the end, the image that kept tugging at me was that of a purple-colored woman, bellowing through time. I didn't know who she was at first, but at some point in the writing process, I realized that the story of Sandra Bland was weighing heavy on my mind and heart and that fragments of her were bleeding into the poem I was piecing together. This dis•articulated poem is for her. When I got to the dis•articulation part of the process I was puzzled by how exactly to reconstruct. I tried just drawing words from your fevered writings onto a note pad, but that wasn't working. I fantasized about breaking up the words in categories (by parts of speech) like I had seen in an example, but that didn't happen. Finally, I enlarged the font of the fevered writings, double-spaced, printed out, and then started to cut and cut. I ended up with strips. It was reminiscent of magnet poetry or sentence strips I have often used with my ESL students. Then it was so much fun! It was like the puzzle on my kitchen table that I kept playing with.

August: Sesshu Foster

Sesshu would like his work to speak for itself.

September: Donna Frazier

I wasn't a stranger to the dis•articulations process. I've sometimes played along when prompts have been posted, and I occasionally look at older entries on the blog when I wanted to start a poem from someplace outside myself. But this time was much more intense. We had a theme to honor. And a place, too—Descanso Gardens *(Editor's Note: Donna and Terry were among a group of poets commissioned to participate in an exhbition, "Oasis," at Descanso Gardens. They decided to use their dis•articulations collaboration to produce poems for that exhibit).* I sat with lists of words, staring at them for long stretches and willing some image of my own to come to mind. I felt a start of deep recognition when Terry posted her free writing here, because I have turned each of those words over and over and over, sometimes willing them to be something else, the perfect word I couldn't have.

I moved Terry's words around, fruitlessly it seemed, until my mind let go and delivered "bird float" and "tree song," and then the words were mine. The poem was there in the unclenching and later in allowing myself to let words and couplets go instead of insisting they stay. This was a difficult, beautiful experience, made all the better by drawing inspiration from the gardens. And the next piece I wrote, with an infinite choice of words, was particularly delicious. I love constraint, and oh how I love releasing myself from it.

October: Ramón García

It was an interesting exercise. The fevered writing in response to Terry's found quotes I approached as a timed stream-of-consciousness experiment. For the writing of the poems from Terry's fevered writing in response to my found quotes, I decided to choose words in the order they were written. This was a method that provided some sense of "form" that intuitively I felt this exercise would benefit from, and I think it did. I also decided not to alter the words in Terry's fevered writing (to not change the tense or make nouns into verbs, etc.); this rule I sensed would support the imagination in choosing the right word for its originality and the structure of the meaning of the poem. It was fun and a great exercise in focusing attention on language and, for me, structuring meaning in a poem.

November: Douglas Kearney

It seems counterintuitive, but receiving a word bank from a collaborator reveals perhaps as much about yourself as it does your accomplice. For me, I kept looking at the list I gleaned from Terry's fevered writings, desperately trying to find the words "down" and "from," prepositions (I think I'm drawn to down as preposition more than as adverb and hardly ever as noun) characteristic of the motions my poems tend to consider. But she gave me "out," which, like down, is mad flavorful as a preposition. The disarticulations project reminds me of the sampling work of J Dilla, and license to chop and reconfigure another poet's writing was a pleasure. I won't risk an attempt to analyze Terry via the words provided, except that one of my favorite alphabetically sequential pairs is "weirdly Western" followed closely by "vulgar wad," while the quartet of "tiptoe to toasty tongues" is messing with my life right now. Even as recomposed by the sort function of Microsoft Word, these combos seem to me imagined by the same writer who turned my fevers into "Janky Mojo." What a generous writer; what a generative experiment!

December: Yvonne M. Estrada

My Dearest Terry,

Well Lovey, thank you for inviting me to play. I have participated in many fevered writing sessions before and have even extracted a few surprising lines for poems. This process was a little different, but the surprise factor was still there. I found it like being given a particular palette of colors to start with and seeing what image would be born. Like any poetic form, the "rules" are what bring on the brainstorm for me, digging deep for the meaning I am after; this brings its own surprise. The freedom to choose any prompt, the freedom to write anything during the fevered writing, and the freedom to reorganize the words in any sequence made dis•articulations an adventure that took me to a poem I didn't know was waiting for me. Bring it on!

Interview: Dis•articulated with Terry Wolverton in the Month of July

by Olga Garcia Echeverría

disarticulate: to make or become disjointed,
as the bones of a body or stems of a plant.

Terry, bienvenida! Can you share what has been the most rewarding part of your dis•articulations 2015 journey so far?

I've had the opportunity to meet and encounter the work of poets I didn't know before (including you!). I've written poems I never would have thought my way to. And I've been told by a couple of collaborating poets that working on the process got them writing again after a dry spell.

What has that been like—working with a different poet each month?

It's just fascinating to study how another poet thinks and how he or she uses language. I worked with one poet whose fevered writing contained no images of the body; that's so different than my own work! Another poet was extravagant with adjectives, which made me aware that I can tend to be sparse. Others used words I would never use in a poem, but I challenged myself to do so. All this is expansive for me (and I hope for the other poets too).

As writers/artists, we have to keep fueling our own visions and creations. What fuels the fire for this particular project?

This project reflects three of my particular loves—a focus on the process of creating (which for me is where art resides), experimentation, and working in community.

The concept of disarticulation seems to be at the heart of your project. What does "disarticulation" mean to you?

The word "disarticulation" literally means to take apart a body, or rather a skeleton—to separate the joints. I borrowed the term because I am taking apart bodies of writing, the passages of fevered writing, and separating them into their component parts of speech—nouns, verbs, adjectives, etc.

It was quite a journey to take apart your fevered writings and play with your words, not knowing where I was going or why I was going there. At times I felt very challenged, but mostly it made me work within certain word boundaries. In the end, I wrote something unexpected and that was really cool. What exactly pulled you into this creative approach?

This process appealed to me because I felt myself falling into familiar ruts with my poetry, returning again and again to certain subject matter, imagery, moods. I wanted a process that would disrupt those patterns; I wanted to surprise myself.

I think a lot of writers can relate to what you are saying about familiar ruts that develop in our writing. I really appreciated the elements of disruption and surprise in the disarticulated exercises. I read on your website that you've done something similar before.

Although I'd been playing with aspects of this process, things came together in 2012; my partner (the poet Yvonne M. Estrada) committed to do fevered writing every day for 30 days; she and I would exchange prompts. She used the results differently to inspire poems, but I began taking apart my fevered writing and recombining it. In 2013 I did a blog project where I invited friends and strangers to give me prompts, and I wrote a new dis•articulations poem every week for a year.

Wow, that is a lot of poetry. It's impressive how you've stuck to the act of disarticulating, and yet you've allowed it to evolve. What contributed to the shift from your blog project in 2013 to dis•articulations 2015?

Working with prompts from other people was great, but I wanted to explore even further disruption, so I had the idea of asking other poets to collaborate, working with poets with a wide variety of poetic styles, disarticulating and reconstructing one another's words to make our poems.

There's a $25 prize for a Reader Poem winner each month, and also collaborating poets are given $50 for their participation. I love this about your project! Are you funding this yourself? And if so, why?

Again, because I'm interested in process and community, I wanted to create a way for others to participate, in addition to the twelve poets I collaborate with. I decided the collaborators would all be Southern California-based, but the readers who submit poems can be anywhere. The $25 prize I had hoped would provide more inspiration to participate; folks who have won the monthly reader poem challenge seem to be pleased with it. Also, I pay the collaborators $50 for their participation; I think poets should get paid, even if it's a nominal fee. I initially wrote a grant for this project, but it wasn't funded, so I had to set aside a little budget to fund it myself on a more modest scale.

This interview was first published on *La Bloga* at http://labloga.blog-spot.com/2015/08/disarticulated-with-terry-wolverton-in.html and was reprinted with permission. © Olga García Encheverría, 2015.

Reader Poem Contributors

Charles Bane, Jr.

Liz Belile

Micki Blenkush

Charles W. Brice

Anthony Ernesto Cepeda

Lisa Cheby

Mellanie Crowell

Dalwyn

Liz Dalwyn

Daniel de Cullá

Jerry García

Olga García Echeverría

Jennifer Hernandez

Trista Hurley-Waxali

Shelly Krehbiel

Henry Medina

Leah Mueller

Eileen Patterson

B.C. Petrakos

Donna Prinzmetal

John Reinhart

Melodic Rose

Shloka Shankar

Cynthia Stewart

Michelle Sydney

Manuel Velez

Sharon Venezio

Tina Yang

About Terry Wolverton

Terry Wolverton is a literary artist and author of ten books of poetry, fiction and creative nonfiction, including *Embers,* a novel in poems, and *Insurgent Muse: life and art at the Woman's Building,* a memoir. She has edited fifteen literary compilations, including (with Robert Drake) three volumes each of *His: brilliant new fiction by gay men* and *Hers: brilliant new fiction by lesbians.* She has also created performance, visual and media arts, and collaborated with choreographers, musicians and visual artists. She is the founder of Writers At Work, a creative writing studio in Los Angeles, and affiliated faculty in the MFA Writing Program of Antioch University Los Angeles. www.terrywolverton.com.

www.ingramcontent.com/pod-product-compliance
Lightning Source LLC
Chambersburg PA
CBHW071542040426
42452CB00008B/1090